Patrick Chukwudezie Chibuko

Liturgy For Life

Patrick Chukwudezie Chibuko

Liturgy For Life

Introduction to Practical Dimensions
of the Liturgy

IKO – Verlag für Interkulturelle Kommunikation

BX
1970
.C52
2005

Bibliographische Information der Deutschen Bibliothek
Die Deutsche Bibliothek verzeichnet diese Publikation in der Deutschen
Nationalbibliographie; detaillierte bibliographische Daten sind im Internet über
http://dnb.ddb.de abrufbar.

©   IKO-Verlag für Interkulturelle Kommunikation
       Frankfurt am Main • London, 2005

       Frankfurt am Main   London
       Postfach 90 04 21   70 c, Wrentham Avenue
       D - 60444 Frankfurt   London NW10 3HG, UK

       e-mail: info@iko-verlag.de • Internet: www.iko-verlag.de

       ISBN: 3-88939-777-8

Umschlaggestaltung: Volker Loschek, 61184 Karben
Herstellung: Bookstation GmbH, 78244 Gottmadingen

TABLE OF CONTENTS

DEDICATION

Rev. Professors:
Peter Damian Akpunonu

and

Anscar J. Chupungco (OSB)
My two greatest mentors

ACKNOWLEDGEMENTS

My profound gratitude goes to Rev. Fr. Joseph Ezechi of the Enugu Diocesan Seminary Staff for his efforts in critically going through the scripts and making very useful corrections and criticisms. I found his comments very insightful.

Rev. Dr. Anthony Egbo of the Theology Department of the Bigard Memorial Seminary Enugu deserves my sincere thanks and gratitude. He calmly and critically went through the work. His constructive corrections and criticisms contributed immensely towards the quality of this work.

Two of the liturgy experts in Nigeria gave their professional touches to this work for which I remain very grateful. I mention with special thanks and appreciation, Rev. Dr. Aloysius Nwabekee of the Chair of Liturgy at the Bigard Memorial Seminary Enugu.

Rev. Dr. Lawrence Madubuko of the Chair of Liturgy at the Blessed Iwene Tansi Major Seminary, Onitsha deserves the greatest expression of thanks and gratitude. He not only went through the work as critical as possible, he also undertook to write the foreword of this work. I do appreciate the foreword as a master piece indeed.

Patrick C. Chibuko
Ash Wednesday,
9th February, 2005.

GENERAL LIST OF ABBREVIATIONS

AA	Acts of the Apostles
AAS	*Acta Apostolicae Sedis. Commentarium Officiale, Typis Polyglottis*, Vatican City, 1909 -
AA.VV	Various Authors
CCC	Catechism of the Catholic Church
CDWDS	Congregation for Divine Worship and the Discipline of the Sacraments
CIC	*Codex Iuris Canonici* (Code of Canon Law), 1983
CEI	*Conferenza Episcopale Italiana*
Cf	Confer
Co.	Company
Col	Letter of St. Paul to the Colossians
Cor	Letter of St. Paul to the Corinthians
CSEL	*Corpus Scriptorum Ecclesiasticorum Latinorum* (Vienna 1866ff)
Eph	Letter of St. Paul to the Ephesians
Esp.	Especially
Etc	*et cetera*
Ex	Exodus
Gal	Letter of St. Paul to the Galatians
GS	*Paulus* PP. V1, *Gaudium et Spes.* AAS 58 (1966)
Heb	Letter to the Hebrews
HIV/AIDS	Human Immuned Virus/Acquired Immuned Deficiency Syndrome
Ibid	*Ibidem*
Jas	Letter of St. James
Jn	Gospel according to St. John
LG	*Lumen Gentium.* Dogmatic Constitution on the Church, 1964

Lk	Gospel according to St. Luke
Matt	Gospel according to St. Matthew
MD	*La Maison-Dieu* (Paris 1945ff)
Mk	Gospel according to Mark
NA	*Nostra Aetate*. Declaration on the Relation of the Church to Non Christian Religions, 1965
NAFDAC	National Administration for Food and Drugs Agency Control (Nigeria)
Neh	Nehemiah
Nr(r)	Number(s)
OLM	*Missale Romanum, Ordo Lectionum Missae* (1969, 1981)
OSB	Order of St. Benedict
Para	Paragraph
Pet	Letter of St. Peter
Phil	Letter of St. Paul to the Philippians
RL	*Rivista Liturgica* (Finalpia/Torino-Leumann 1914ss)
Rom	Letter of St. Paul to the Romans
RS	*Redemptionis Sacramentum*
RSV	Revised Standard Version
SC	*Sacrosanctum Concilium*, The Constitution on the Sacred Liturgy, 1963
SCR	Sacred Congregation for Rites
SChr	Sources Chretiennes
SNAAP	Famous Publishing Co. in Enugu, Nigeria
SPCK	Famous Publishing Co. in London, England
Tim	Letter of St. Paul to Timothy
Trans	Translator/ion
USCCB	United States Conference of Catholic Bishops
Zech	Prophet Zechariah

FOREWORD

Fr. Patrick Chibuko's work is an anthology of liturgical essays. It comprises five essays prefaced with a general introduction and ended with a general conclusion. The readers used to our author's writings will meet in this volume some themes which can safely be described as pets of Fr. P. Chibuko.

There are, apart from his emphasis on the liturgical centrality of the paschal mystery of Christ, the affirmation that liturgical experience has ethico-political implications. In an inspiring summary on a section on liturgical spirituality he writes: liturgy well celebrated and understood has the great potentiality to assess any given situation in its proper perspective, instil courage into fainting hearts, provide courage in the midst of doubt and able to create practical options in the midst of diminishing alternatives.

More specifically, he concludes that it is incongruent to announce in the Eucharist that the risen Christ gives himself in food and drink for the nourishment of the world and have no concern for the millions who die for want of nourishment. Thus, liturgical celebration binds the christian to act in a certain way. It implies an ethics inclusive of mission and social justice.

Fr. Chibuko's present volume, however, is not simply a refurbishing of old tools. In the first chapter he presents an insight which, if not altogether new, at least is a refreshing articulation. Here the author makes the point that there is a significant diversity in the respective structures of Western and African ritual. This is borne out by anthropological studies of Igbo religion and culture. With relevance to the structure of the Igbo ritual of prayer Francis Cardinal Arinze had noted that in public prayer the priest or leader leads, and the people repeat after him, or the people may give their hearty approbation only at each requ-est. If the priest forgets anything the men present may remind him.

What Arinze noted in the area of praying Onuora Enekwe corroborates in his study of Igbo dance. According to Enekwe, whereas it would be unthink-able for spectators in a theatre in the western world to interfere with a performance, in African context, specifically in the Igbo setting, it is most legitimate and indeed desirable that spectators show their appreciation of the performance, not only by sticking money on the performers like dancers but also doing some initiation of the performers while the session is still on. It can only be imagined what can be the consequences for liturgy in Igboland of giving due recognition to this diversity between the structures of ritual in the West and in Africa.

The author also presents an interesting study on liturgical homily. That is in the fifth and last chapter. This is a great service to our local ecclesial community as it set out the specificity of the liturgical homily, distinguishing it, that is, from various other modalities of presenting the Word of God, by the Church.

Perhaps one of the greatest features of this work, likely to be glossed over by a casual reader is the author's disciplined way of keeping his conclusions within the bounds of evidence. For instance, he duly notes on the one hand, the magisterial teaching that homilies are reserved to the hierarchy or the ordained ministers in the church and, on the other hand, he equally notes that the evidence of history is less than apodictic on the issue. This is a feature that is not characteristic of the writings by African scholars as a class and the absence of which had made the international scholarly world, regrettable but justifiably, refer to such works as lacking in intellectual rigour.

The work includes a chapter on the history of the Eucharist across the ages. Against the background of the author's presentation of the Eucharist as the constant and the rallying factor of the Church his high-lighting some specific areas in liturgy that raise concern make sense. He hints that genuine liturgical inculturation is imperative if liturgy is to be permanently relevant.

In this volume, Fr. Chibuko has put in the hands of the local church, especially, those who are on the drivers' seat, a useful implement for work - an *instrumentum laboris*.

Lawrence Madubuko (Rev. Fr. Dr.)

Chair of Liturgy

Blessed Iwene Tansi Major Seminary, Onitsha.

LITURGY FOR LIFE
Introduction to Practical Dimensions of the Liturgy

GENERAL INTRODUCTION

The encyclical *Mediator Dei*, defines Liturgy as the public worship which our Redeemer as the head of the Church renders to the Father, as well as the worship which the community of the faithful renders to its Founder, and through him to the heavenly Father. In short, it is the worship rendered by the Mystical Body of Christ in the entirety of its head and members.[1] This classical definition has indeed influenced profoundly the definition of the liturgy by the reformed liturgy of the Second Vatican Council,[2] *Sacrosanctum Concilium* which presents the liturgy as an exercise of the priestly office of Jesus Christ, as the whole public worship performed by the Mystical Body of Jesus Christ, that is, by the Head and his members, and as an action of Christ the Priest and of his Body which is the Church.[3]

Within the context of this definition by SC., there is the basic concept of the presence of Christ in the celebrations of the Mass, the Sacraments, the Word of God and the Divine Office. At Mass for instance, Christ himself, now offers through the hands of the priests, who formerly offered himself on the cross. In effect, when a person baptises it is really Christ himself who baptises. He is present in the proclamation of the Word and when the Church prays and sings. All these affirmations underline the active role played by Christ in the exercise of his priestly office, an exercise which he performed as he preached the good news, healed the sick, freed those in bondage, and culminated by his death on the cross, resurrection from the dead and bestowal of the Holy Spirit.[4]

Liturgy definitely goes beyond the mere celebration of the sacraments or even the sole celebration of the Eucharist. The reformed liturgy of the Second Vatican Council instructs that the sacred liturgy does not exhaust the entire activity of the Church[5]. Nevertheless, the liturgy is the (*culmen et fons*) summit toward which the activity of the Church is directed; at the same time the fount or source from which all the Church's power flows.[6] The christian activities are not restricted only to the celebration of the sacraments or the Eucharist alone, but rather include all the legitimate activities which christians engage themselves in, spiritual, social, economic, political, human, personal, national, international relationships etc. All these in effect are to have their summit and source in the liturgy that is celebrated for the celebration to be relevant to the Church and to the larger society.

As a matter of fact, the liturgy celebrates the core salvific mystery of the Christ namely, the paschal mystery whose transformative and tremendous effects spread across all human concerns. The paschal mystery of Christ in the broad sense comprises the totality of the life of Christ starting from the incarnation and stretching through the passion, death and resurrection, sitting at the right hand of the Father, to the final coming of Christ in glory. In the strict sense, paschal mystery refers to the passion, death and resurrection of Christ.

Furthermore, the liturgy facilitates the re-enactment of this redemptive mystery of Christ and makes it relevant to all people at all time. The liturgy has the capacity to spread across the fruits of the celebration to become really the source and summit of all christian activities. The world in which the christian finds himself, falls within the scope of the liturgical celebrations. Liturgical celebrations thus, become a kind of catalyst, inspirator and motivating force that determines the complete way of life of the christian where ever he or she finds him or herself.

Paradoxically, the liturgy which the church celebrates has an open door policy but at the same time, it is exclusive. Here everyone is invited to participate although in varying degrees. Everyone is cordially welcomed to the celebration. All are enjoined to participate as far as they can. This gives the liturgical celebration the universal outlook which it has. For as many as enter to share in the celebration are called by God to enjoy the benefits of being the children of God. The children of God are entitled to hear the word of God, to receive the blessings of God, to fellowship with other children of God and to share in the body and blood of Christ by those who have attained such a level of christian formation. As often as all participate, they are encouraged to follow the various stages of growth and formation through liturgical catechesis.

The all embracing nature of the liturgy presupposes the need for the creation of appropriate rites and rituals for an effective celebration of the liturgy. The paschal mystery which Christ entrusted to the Church ought to be celebrated for the transformation of the members, sanctification and edification of the Church leading to the ultimate glorification of God through witness of life. In many positive ways, the liturgical reforms of the Second Vatican Council have attempted to achieve this noble and ultimate objective. The reform could be said to have succeeded in doing this by restoring the Roman rite back to its pristine simplicity, brevity, sobriety, and clarity. Secondly, the reform's insistence on full, conscious and active participation in the liturgy is aimed at a meaningful celebration of the paschal mystery of Christ.[7] Flexibility through the process of pluralism in the liturgy was the undercurrent of the reformed liturgy.[8] The liturgical reformers however, underscored the limitations of the Roman rite especially with regard to its inability to satisfy the sentiments of different people in their cultural backgrounds as well as the social changes in human life. It therefore created rooms for the enrichment of the Roman rite with the authentic cultural values and the genius of the people.

The Council demands the creation of liturgical forms which will be imbued with the cultural values and the genius of the people. The Council insists that, while restoring the liturgy to the reach of people's comprehension, active and full participation, both texts and rites should be drawn up so as to express more clearly the holy things which they signify. The Christian people, as far as possible, should be able to understand them with ease and take part in them fully, actively and as a community.[9]

It further maintains that the Church earnestly desires that Christ's faithful, when present at the mystery of faith, should not be there as strangers or silent spectators. On the contrary, through a good understanding of the rites and prayers they should take part in the sacred action, conscious of what they are doing, with devotion and full collaboration. They should be instructed by God's word, and be nourished at the table of the Lord's Body. They should give thanks to God, offering the immaculate victim, not only through the hands of the priest but also together with him, they should learn to offer themselves.[10] The challenging recommendations of the reformed liturgy of the Second Vatican Council could well be seen as an urgent call to go back to local cultures to find suitable values within the cultures to enrich the christian rites or even to create entirely new rites.

The recommendation of the Council portrays the liberal mind of the Fathers of the reformed liturgy to encourage varieties in the church's worshipping forms.[11] These varieties resulting ultimately to different practices pertaining to the liturgy, the divergent applications, the juridical and administrative norms proper to local churches cumulatively lead to the emergence of liturgical rites. Rite in this sense therefore, does not simply apply to a single action, for example, sacramental administration. Rather, it touches all expressions of the faith particular to a local Church.[12] In this broad sense of the term rite, liturgy becomes an integral part that makes up the totality of the life pattern of a people. Such a creation is the challenge to the local Churches to provide the people with an authentic liturgy which would be truly christian and fully cultural.[13]

Liturgy presupposes in addition functional structures of rituals which exhibit an extensive and critiqued people's way of life which will be integrated into their worshipping forms as their authentic cultural values and genius. At the same time, such practical rituals need to show openness to new ideas, new orientations, new possibilities, innovations especially with regard to the changing values of the society. Rules and creativity become in this context, the hallmark of constitutive structures of rituals.

Liturgy for life demands also a liturgical vision which will underscore the solidarity of all peoples excluding no one in the body of Christ and beyond. The cosmic Christ is the redeemer of all, both believers and non-believers. He is the King of kings, the Lord of the universe, the *Alpha* and the *Omega*, the finisher of the christian faith. He is the One in whom all creation move and have their being. The Lord to whom all creation tend towards as their end. The liturgy incorporates all that in the celebration and makes it a reality in the daily life of the people.

To accomplish this great global objective, liturgy will continue to make a constant return to the narrative logic of ritual *anamnesis*. Actually in the rites composed of words, gestures and sometimes material elements the Church recalls or makes an *anamnesis* of what God the Father has accomplished through Christ in human salvation. The act of recalling, of calling to mind, of making present is basic in the nature of the liturgy for life. It is through anamnesis that God's marvellous deeds, the *Magnalia Dei*, are recalled by the liturgical ass-embly and are made present in their midst.[14]

Through anamnesis the worshippers are enabled to experience in their lives God's work of salvation. The celebration of the Eucharist and the Sacraments is thus always an *anamnesis* of God's saving work, a presence in ritual form, and an experience of faith.[15]

A single event in the life of Christ which constitutes the core of liturgical celebration cannot be left to the chances of memories. For there are certain events in life which cannot be allowed to pass by without recalling it daily, weekly, yearly indeed, at every moment of life because of the great difference it makes in the life of the people both for believers and believers in potency. The ritual *anamnesis* with its transformative potentialities cuts across individuals, collective groups, gender, race, creed, colour and other possible barriers. Certainly not every event in the life of humans qualify to be rem-embered in a celebration form as the ritual *anamnesis* of the Lord's paschal mystery.

Anamnesis leads to *Epiclesis*. *Epiclesis* completes the action of *anamnesis*. The two concepts are related to each other in much the same way as the paschal mystery and the mystery of Pentecost. Just as the bestowal of the Holy Spirit on the Church on the day of Pentecost culminates Christ's saving work in his death and resurrection, so does the prayer of *epiclesis* culminate the action of *anamnesis*. When the Church recalls God's marvellous deeds in Christ, it also prays for the bestowal of the Holy Spirit who will consecrate or make holy the people and the sacramental elements used in worship. In the liturgy we not only recall the paschal mystery of Christ, we also receive the Holy Spirit.[16]

Liturgy for life makes a clarion call for an authentic and radical *epiclesis* of life. Liturgy for life must be lived under the unction of the Holy Spirit. The Spirit of God motivates, inspires and puts into constant flame the liturgical spirituality which is actually synonymous with liturgy for life in overtures.

Perhaps this explains the rationale for exploring all possibilities within the limits of the means available to the Church to make liturgical celebrations ever more relevant to the people in their given cultural backgrounds. Attendance to the eucharistic celebration for instance, ought to be done with all amount of excellence in all scores.[17]

One of the excellent features of the liturgy for life, would be to make the liturgy a privileged space where the oppressor and the oppressed share a common table of God's Word and Sacraments. The result of which would be a clear realisation of the enormity of the wounds and injustice on the part of the oppressor which move one to true redress and sincere reconciliation. On the other hand, the oppressed sees the need to manifest that gift of God to forgive and forget even though the oppressor knew exactly what he or she was doing.[18]

Against this backdrop, those who receive the true Body of Christ become really the mystical Body of Christ. One banquet in this case, effects a wonderful and practical change. The liturgy furthermore becomes the celebration space where the well-fed and the undernourished share a common table resulting in the concern for the poor and equitable justice for all the victims of injustice everywhere.

It needs further to be re-iterated for the sake of emphasis, that the functionality of liturgy for life depends a great deal on the appreciation of the gift of diversities in liturgical celebrations. Liturgy naturally becomes rather mono-tonous when and where everyone in the world is meant to do one thing in only one way. Diversity is a gift of the Spirit which is meant to create a healthy variety which is described as the spice of life.

The various forms of diversity in the Church should be seen from the positive perspective, as long as one maintains the substantial unity of the faith, the formal expression of the faith must not be uniform.[19] The Church in this case favours unity in diversity, oneness in plurality. Individual and particular practices if well co-ordinated do not introduce confusion, instead they display the vest of many colours that make up the unity of the Body of Christ.[20]

Against this background, liturgy for life will be examined under the following headings as chapters with sub-chapters: structures of rituals, rules and creativity as basic in the search for a homely and practical liturgy; liturgical spirituality as prerequisite for qualitative life; the divine eucharistic commission to win disciples for Christ as practical means of reaching out to all with the good news of salvation for all; the undying hope of the Church in the eucharistic liturgy as an inevitable source of nourishment for the life that one discovers in the liturgy and the role of liturgical preaching as most efficient means of communication in favour of liturgy for life.

CHAPTER ONE:

Structures of Rituals: Rules and Creativity

i.   Introduction

Structures of rituals, rules and creativity intend to review the phenomenon of divination and the role of diviners as indispensable determining factors in evolving soothing structures of rituals for every life's conflict and its resolution within the context of African Traditional Religion. The African christian finds himself or herself in two worlds, thus giving rise to two different structures of rituals: African Structures of Rituals and the Christian Structures of Rituals. These will be reviewed against the backdrop of the over all aim of this work, liturgy for life.[21]

The result of the review logically brings one to the crux of the matter namely, the compatibility or the incompatibility of rules and creativity in relation to the evolution of dynamic structures of rituals. In evolving structures of rituals, in what sense can rules and creativity be understood and rightly applied? Can one deal with rules in the strict sense of closeness which admits of no flexibility or creativity? Do rules include or make room for creativity? Is creativity possible without rules? What are the limits of each?

The reformed liturgy of the Second Vatican Council has challenged itself and the world under the classical Roman Rite to make a good blend of rules and creativity in their ritual celebrations. What reactions emerge in response to this from various peoples within their backgrounds and cultural milieu?

ii.   Structures of Ritual in African Traditional Religion

Rituals in African Traditional Religion are often determined from case to case. Each case determines its own Ritual structure. Existentialists, phenomenologists, pragmatists and so on, believe that ritual emerges through trial and error as an answer to existential questions. It originates as an action that installs order into chaos, the chaos of estrangement and human life-questioning.

Hence people regard ritual as a regulated gesture acquired by way of gesticulation or through making blind affirmations. Through this process, human beings finally succeed in inventing adequate gestures to pacify their distress in the universe.[22] The scope of ritual is both for a group or individual.

The social group goes through a learning process to arrive at adequate rituals that confirm its particular insertion into the world. The acquired social and religious rituals become the media of interaction and further creativity in the universe despite the rigid or repetitive pattern of ritual action.

The determinant factor of the ritual in each case rests squarely on the diviner both for the social group and individual. It belongs to his divination ministry to do a lot of listening. He or she would be required to listen attentively to each case, relays the case to the gods by way of consultation to the gods and obtains from the gods what sort of ritual elements are required and sometimes even the ritual structures to be followed. The ritual structures emerge as an aftermath of the listening process and due consultations with the gods. Only then can the most applicable, functional and satisfactory ritual structures be determined.

In other words, no one ritual structure applies to all cases even when the cases appear similar. For instance, in a case of childless marriage, the childless couple would consult the diviner, narrate their story. As the diviner listens attentively to the distress story he could punctuate it with interrogations. On consulting the gods with the story, he or she listens again attentively to what the gods would have to say as being responsible for their childlessness. The oracle of the diviner as a response from the god, could be that the god of fertility is angry with the couple as a result of certain crime committed by someone in their lineage in the past. It could be that the family failed to kill a cow for their long diseased forefather of the husband or wife. And so in angry and retaliatory reaction, the forefather has closed the womb of the woman or rendered the husband temporarily sterile or even impotent. The result of the consultation would be a prescription of the ceremony (rite) to be performed with the detailed series of actions within the rite to be performed (ritual) as it relates to the case of failure to give their forefather a befitting funeral rite by killing a cow for him.

For another childless couple, the cause of their crisis could be as a result of a crime committed by the family in the past, like selling one of their family members into slavery and so the gods are angry and crying for proper redress. To appease the same god of fertility different rituals could be prescribed. Even the same case could be presented to the different diviners and their results would lead to different ritual prescriptions. In effect, rituals and their structures in African Traditional context have greater tendencies in creating ample room for accommodation. They are mostly distinguished by creativity, relativity, flexibility and fluidity.

Every ritual gesture is a symbolic action or a ritual symbol. The symbol is the smallest unit of ritual which still retains its specific properties of ritual behaviour.[23] As a symbol, the ritual generates group identity. It becomes a kind of code through which a particular group expresses its insertion into the world. It may thus reveal the very heart of a society. Furthermore, the aspect of repetition, which is a fundamental property of ritual gesture, translates ritual behaviour into an instrument of social engineering: it stipulates a certain way of acting, and because of its rigid or conservative nature, it possesses the quality of revealing the structures that found a particular social group.[24]

iii.   Divination in African Traditional Religion

In dealing with African rituals one has first to consider what kinds of circumstances that tend to give rise to ritual performances, for these circumstances probably decide what sort of rituals to be performed and the goals of that ritual largely determine also the meaning of symbols to be used in it. The switch-point (the diviner or celebrant) between social crises (that occasioned the need for rituals) and performance of redressive ritual is the divinatory seance or consultation. First there is a crisis. Second there is the diviner. Third, the listening process by the diviner to the story of the distressed clients. Fourth, the consultation of the gods by the diviner with the story contents and finally there is a redressive ritual prescription.

It was Victor Turner who maintained that divination has certain affinities with the judicial process for it is virtually concerned with the customs and interests of persons in complex social situations. But it also prepares the way for the more rigidly standardised processes of redressive ritual. It is this mediating function that determines the cognitive and flexible qualities of its symbolism.[25]

In African context, performances of rite are seen in terms of such concepts as social fields, process, situation, social drama, conflict, the difference between repetitive and radical change etc. Here rituals are seen as concatenation of symbols and systems of values, beliefs and meanings. These two order of things are not identical because, the particular form one of them takes does not directly imply the form the other will take. There may be discrepancy and even tension, between them in particular situations, notably in those dominated by rapid social change.[26]

iv.   Diviner's Role in African Traditional Religion

Among African social groups like *Ndembu* people, the Diviner regards his tasks as very practical in terms of revealing the causes of misfortune or death. These are almost invariably mystical or non-empirical in character, although human wishes, desires and feeling are involved. The Diviners disclose what has happened and do not foretell future events. In some places they are seldom oracular or mantic. They do not inaugurate the divinatory process, but wait until clients come to consult them. Modes of divination are regarded as instruments which both detect lies and discover truth, although, since they are operated by fallible men, their verdicts are not always accepted without question. For witches are accredited with extra-ordinary powers of deception and even great diviners fortify themselves with special medicines to combat the deceits and illusions sent by their secret antagonists to baffle them. One such medicine is used at the first stage of a consultation.

The diviner occupies a central position with reference to several fields of social and cultural relationships. He acts as a mechanism of redress and social adjustment in the field of local descent groups, since he locates areas and point of tension in their contemporary structures. He exonerates or accuses individuals in those groups in terms of a system of moral norms. Since he operates in emotionally charged situations, such norms are restated in striking and memorable fashion. Thus he may be said to play a vital role in upholding tribal morality. Moral law is most vividly made known through its breach.

The diviner's role is pivotal to the system of rituals of affliction, anti witchcraft- sorcery rituals, since he decides what kind of ritual should be performed in a given instance, when it should be performed and sometimes who should perform it. Since diviners are consulted on many occasions, it is clear that their role as upholders of tribal morality and rectifiers of disturbed social relationships, both structural and contingent is a vital one in a society without centralised political institutions.[27]

On account of the virtue of their extra-ordinary sensitivity to spiritual reality and years of training, they are referred to as fathers of secrets. They are able to decipher the past, the present and the future as well as to uncover the human and spiritual causes of events and the possible solutions to the problems of life.[28] For many Africans, the diviners form a bridge between the human world and the world of spirits. Due to their special contact with the spiritual powers, messages are received through them from the other world, or men are given knowledge of things that would otherwise be difficult to know. As such, they are looked upon as men with highly sensitive faculties.[29] They are consulted and respected for solving the riddles of life and ensuring a measure of certainty.[30]

In another development, their functions include the following: if anything is lost, if a barren woman desires children, if there is a mysterious disease, if a man is troubled by strange dreams, and for many other causes, the diviner is sought out and has recourse to geomancy. The diviner may be called in at all the important crises of life, at birth to discover the appropriate name to give a child, at the betrothal to find the right husband, at death to find who has caused it. In some places the diviner draws up a horoscope for adolescents, and this is treasured by them the rest of their life as showing their fate. The horoscope is inscribed on a piece of calabash and any competent diviner should be able to read it.[31]

The role of diviners seen against this background may be very unrealistic, since there are many unsolved riddles of life in Africa as there are many barren women. But it may not be right to say that divination is simply a trick and not a religious practice or a science because of the many problems noticeable in many African societies. While it is possible that diviners may fail from time to time, it is also possible that some seem to have powers of telepathy[32] because they appear to be able to tell the client facts about himself or herself and the purpose of his visit at the very start of the interview.[33] The diviners are very clever and intelligent type of people who are said to have inherited the ability of divination from their fathers or is specially chosen and trained by the divinity of divination to become its medium for unravelling the riddles of life.

Although the *Turkana* (Kenya) diviners are said to receive prophetic dreams and foretell the future, they are not prophets. Rather, they could be compared with the *Meru* religious leader (the *Mugwe*) who is said to derive his power from God. The diviners are spoken of as the children of God or people of God. They are regarded as the link between men and God. They are like the *Meru* religious leaders who are considered as wise men, men of God, the chiefs, the leaders and the saviours who have led their people away from their former land of bondage. Because *Mugwe* is said to know and teach about God, his calling is believed to come from God. He becomes God's messenger as well as representing the people's needs before God. In addition, he is the tutor of young initiates and the guarantor of the society's prosperity. He is like the father of the *Meru*, because he prays for his people. Not only that he is regarded as a man of God, but that he is identified with God.[34] Notwithstanding that there are some diviners who combine divination by manipulation apparatus with divination by spirit-possession, the diviner is thus a social as well as moral analyst who by linking misfortunes to breaches of social and moral norms, significantly contributes in sustaining the moral and social values of the society.[35]

Among the chief rituals evolved by the diviners include: redressive rituals, life crisis rituals, rituals of affliction etc. All rituals of affliction for instance are preceded by some recourse to divination, however perfunctory and it is in the divinatory process that quarrels, competition and alignments among people are brought to light.[36]

v. Two Structures of Rituals in Review

a. African Religion

The African ritual structure is hardly defined as every case is treated on its own merit. No particular ritual has a general usage or application. African ritual structures enjoys the latitude of being fluid, free from specific guidelines that must be followed each time. For instance, the following structures or steps were adopted in the case of the clan that was confronted with an economic and political problem. Legal processes were available to resolve the issue according to native law and custom. But the cost of the legal process threw the clan into a crisis. It was normal for the clan-chief to convoke an assembly and normal for him to lay the problem at the feet of the clan ancestors, namely,

i.   convocation of the assembly by the clan chief (the ancestral representation) chief priest of the clan

ii. pouring of libation and offering of the kola nut (gesture of communion)

iii. invocation of the ancestors by the chief, who pleaded with the gods to intervene in favour of their descendants

iv. awaiting the reaction of the ancestors who replied through a dream

v.   victory celebrations in which the renewal of the life of the community tied to the ever present ancestors was ritually displayed.[37]

This ritual process or structure is the popular pattern in the Central African region where ancestral cult is very strong. In other places the principal spirits that may be involved in such a crisis vary. For instance, among *Ndigbo* (Nigeria), though ancestors will be involved, *Ala* (the earth deity who presides over the land and over law and order) will be prominent. But it is a common practice to convoke a religious assembly involving the community or a cross section of it to resolve issues affecting everyday life. In this way life is lived under the eyes of God and the spirits.

In Central African region like Congo, the invocation of the ancestors and their miraculous answer renewed the community and assured it of the presence of its spiritual founders. It is the awareness of this presence that guides life in the present and shapes it for the future. The material need of the land ensures well-being to the living and the living-dead. The possession of the land (which is also spiritualised) also guarantees the survival of the memory of the ancestors with whom the living keep daily communion through prayers and libations. For the land of the living and that of the ancestors, though different, are warmly linked.[38]

The African culture has great tendency towards spontaneity, creativity, accommodation and inculturation. For the exuberant Africans the precision and brevity of the western ritual structure will hit them flat and anaemic. The multi-purpose ritual structure of the west would impact little or nothing in their worshipping forms.

Perhaps the search for authentic and mutual complementarity of the Western Rite with all the families that belong to the Roman Ritual bloc explains the motive, spirit, vision and thrust of the Fathers of the Second Vatican Council in their liturgical reforms. Another word for this search is liturgical inculturation.

b. Christian Religion

Christian rituals have the general tendency to being a clearly worked out structure with general application to all similar cases. The detailed logistics as mentioned above in the African ritual structures are not often existent.The celebrant in this case has only to lend his voice to what is already clearly stated with little or nothing to add or to subtract. Creativity in the sense of initiative tends to be lost here.

Secondly, the Western culture which is largely christian favours a great deal of simplicity, brevity, sobriety and precision in their structures of rituals. Rigidity and fixity marked for instance, the ritual structures of the Tridentine and Post Tridentine forms of worship. One of course can understand the background from which the Tridentine publications were coming from.

The fruits of the reformed liturgy of the Second Vatican Council seen in the publications of the official liturgical books were a big stride not only to mitigate the rigidity of Trent, but also to underscore the simplicity, brevity, sobriety and precision of the West and above all giving room to creativity although under certain rules, principles, guidelines and instructions. *De Benedictionibus* for instance has series of blessings for various states in the life of the people.

A particular ritual suffices for a group of cases with similar contents. For instance, one would be made to use a particular ritual in dealing with all barren women. A particular ritual is structured to serve the needs of farmers seeking bumper harvest. A particular ritual structure is followed to celebrate thanksgiving of all types etc.

Again in the Missale Romanum of Paul V1 that emerged after the Second Vatican Council (1970 *Editio Typica*; 1975 *Editio Typica Altera*; and 2000 *Editio Typica Tersa*) the section on Ritual Masses, Votive Masses and (*Varii Necessitatibus*) Masses for the Various Needs of the People speak volumes of the Western traits in the structures of rituals.

vi. African Structures of Rituals and Christian Structures of Rituals - A Case of Rules and Creativity

A critical review of the two ritual structures well indicates the deficiencies in each requiring an authentic and mutual complementarity. The positive values in one should make up the lacunae in the other especially in this new era of liturgical inculturation. The need for authentic and mutual complementarity of ritual structures today cannot be over stressed. Owing to their different backgrounds, there exists a seeming tension between the two structures of rituals. Openness to change (as is characteristic of the Igbo world view) and acceptance of the elasticity of knowledge (as is characteristic in the Yoruba *ifa* divination) not only indicate another point of view, but are all taken up into the rhythm of the social group's ritual.

Of the two ritual structures, one appears to be rules oriented (Christian ritual structure) and the other seems to be creativity oriented (African ritual structures), hence the apparent anti-thesis of closeness and openness; codification and accommodation; constantly fixed and variation; documentation and spontaneity; exclusiveness and inclusiveness; fixity and fluidity; formalism and freedom; generalisation and particularity; impersonality and personal touch; insensitivity and sensitivity; law of the head and law of the heart; legalism and the laws of the land; rationalisation and intuition; rigidity and elasticity; routine and initiative; rubricism and randomness; staticism and dynamism; inertia and growth; stereo-typed and innovation oriented; uniform-ity and plurality in the two structures.

Rules definitely are necessary for the sake of order, consistency and orthodoxy. Rules like laws are part and parcel of human life and development. Without rules and laws chaos and confusion abound especially in matters of worship. Imagine what worship especially in the Church would have been without the liturgical instructions. The church is even very careful to use more of instructions than rules and laws. Where it uses laws and rules they are not as penally binding as canonical laws and other human laws. Liturgical rules are like the laws of Christ, which are essentially life oriented, encapsulated in the law of love. For law is meant for man and not man for law. Secondly, if there was anything Christ fought against during his sojourn on earth it was the empty ritualism and rigid legalism of his contemporaries. Rules are meaningful in so far as they serve the ultimate purpose of the people. Rules must be at the service of the people for whom they were made and not vice versa.

Rules are to creativity what they are to life. Rules regulate life for the sake of order, consistency, mutual co-existence and general welfare of all. Inasmuch as rules are necessary for life, they form rather part and parcel of life. Life transcends rules. Life is larger than rules. Rules find their raison d'être in life. Rules in isolation from life have no meaning. The elasticity of life therefore diminishes the rigidity of rules. The dynamism in life exposes the hollowness in legalism. Life indeed gives flesh and heart to rules. Structures of rituals which are dehydrated of human feelings, of human needs, their aspirations, or impairs their personal and deep encounter with God and with fellow human beings need to be reviewed in the light of this discussion.

Against this backdrop, creativity like life needs rules. Creativity does not exclude rules but the rules must be understood within a ritual context. Creativity abhors random and haphazard approach. Creativity is not a solemn installation of anarchy or lawlessness in ritual action. Creativity makes no open decla-ration for a wholesale cultural imposition which may be alien to the people or a wholesale imperial colonial imposition. For creativity to be meaningful, conscientious efforts must be made to understand and properly apply certain principles or rules. In actual fact, any meaningful and constructive structures of rituals must necessarily exhibit a reasonable measure of consistency and order. Thus within the context of the principles, rules and order the essentials of such a structure become easily discernible, comprehensible and easy to be followed not only by the people concerned but even by outsiders who belong to the same confession but rather in a more universal context.

Strictly speaking, creativity follows certain rules but at the same time transcends the limits of strict or rigid rules. Rules are thus at the service of creativity especially in the context of structures of rituals. Creativity mitigates the rigidity of rules. Creativity gives flesh and heart also to rules to make them human. Creativity supplies the milk of human heart to the sternness of rules in the structures of rituals. Rules and creativity therefore, are not dialectically opposed to each other, but mutually complementary. Rules are to be followed but with openness to new initiatives, new orientations, new situations, individual cases, new circumstances and innovations. Rules without openness to creativity tantamounts to empty legalism while creativity without rules places structures of rituals on the fast lane to annihilation and nullity. Therefore, one can make bold to say that rules need creativity and creativity demands rules. One would rightly think that this is the balance which the reformed liturgy of the Second Vatican Council wishes to strike in her whole attempt and effort at liturgical inculturation with Anscar J. Chupungco as one of the chief protagonists.

vii.   Rules and Creativity According to the Reformed Liturgy of the Second Vatican Council

It must however be observed, that although liturgical questions were not thoroughly examined within their full cultural contexts, *Sacrosanctum Concilium*, the Constitution on the liturgy is the first document that the Second Vatican Council issued. In the document, it is clearly stated that, in the liturgy, the Church has no wish to impose a rigid uniformity in matters which do not involve the faith or the good of the whole community. Rather she respects and fosters the spiritual adornments and gifts of the various races.[39] Hence the call for plurality or diversity and not uniformity in worship.

The same Council in the next chapter however, mentioned what could be described as putting a hurdle for innovations and creativity in liturgical renewal when it says: Provided that the substantial unity of the Roman rite is maintained, the revision of liturgical books should allow for legitimate variations and adaptations to different groups, regions, and peoples, especially in mission lands.[40] It is indeed hard to see how one can speak of authentic African rites which would maintain the substantial unity of the Roman rite. It is equally hard to see how the Council intends to respect and foster the spiritual adornments and gifts of the various races and peoples, when this exercise is limited to variations and adaptations of the reformed Roman liturgical books.[41]

Against this backdrop, conscientious attempts would be made to transcend this restrictive principle of revision, variations and adaptation to deal with radical adaptation that is today referred to as inculturation which essentially consists in the encounter between Christ *in toto* and the authentic values of the people, giving birth to a new Christian-African way of life. The christian mystery needs to be at home in the life of the people and the cultural values need to be fully integrated within the frame work of the saving mysteries of Christ.

One is however consoled when the same Council spoke of new local rites growing organically from the Roman Rite. This could be the sense in which the courageous Zairian Episcopal Conference talks about the Zairian Mass of the Roman Rite in the form of a daughter growing organically from the mother. In this case, the Zairian Mass grows from the mother Roman Rite.

E. E. Uzukwu confirms this when he said, in Zaire, the Roman Missal for the use of the dioceses of Zaire is normally referred to as the Zairian rite. The rite as it is used here is wider than the eucharistic celebration. It covers all the liturgical, theological and disciplinary patterns found in the church of Zaire. Consequently, a Zairian rite is still in the making. But since the Eucharist is the focal point of the church's life, the officially approved Zairian Mass is a sign of a new rite in an advanced stage.[42]

The essential elements and helpful perspectives for the first criterion of liturgy says that, the Catholic Church rejects nothing of what is true and holy in these non-Christian Religions. She has a high regard for the manner of life and conduct, the precepts and doctrines which, although differing in many ways from her own teaching, nevertheless often reflect a ray of that truth which enlightens all people. Yet she proclaims and is duty bound to proclaim without fail, Christ who is the way, the truth and the life (Jn. 14:6). In him, in whom

God reconciled all things to Himself (2 Cor. 5:18-19), men and women find the fullness of their religious life.[43]

Be that as it may, the reformed Liturgy of the Second Vatican Council took very bold steps to accommodate the great values found in other religions. The Church regards these values as complementary to what she has already and at the same time indicates her openness to enrich itself with those values for an emergent and eventual ritual celebration that would be truly christian and fully cultural.

viii.   The Celebrant in the Reformed Liturgy of the Second Vatican Council

It could well be said that the primary objective of the Fathers of the Reformed Liturgy of the Second Vatican Council is to make every celebrant a liturgist. By being a liturgist in this context means, one who like a professional actor in the theatre enters into the spirit of the major character of the play or drama. The self is forgotten while the main actor (Christ) is being staged. So also the liturgist or celebrant of the reformed liturgy would have to enter fully into the spirit of the liturgy dramatising no longer himself but the chief actor in the ritual celebration. The worshipping community would see itself well situated within the saving mysteries of Christ with the ultimate result of radical transformation of the assembly unto sanctification, edification and glorification of God through witness of life. Secondly, the celebrant would be able to carry everyone along in the ritual celebration leading to what the Fathers referred to as active, conscious and full participation.

As it were, this would be the aim of the liturgical reforms as well as the general norm for all who belong to the classical Roman Rite. Different people have received this general norm differently following their cultural contexts. For the Western world under the Roman Rite, the response follows along their cultural background which is principally serene with almost zero exuberance and enthusiasm in expression. They appear to be contented with already worked out, documented and codified ritual structures as well contained in the official liturgical books. The structures of rituals for various celebrations as contained in the official books are satisfactory and are to be followed religiously. The celebrant has only to lend his voice to the stipulated ritual structures with no addition or subtraction. Faithful observance of the ritual structures would consist of *anamnesis*, re-enactment, *mimesis*, imitation through *martyria,* witness of life.

ix. Aspects of *Anamnesis-Mimesis-Metasxesis-Martyria* in Worship

The African response also follows their cultural background which of course is different from the Western background mentioned above. Already worked out ritual structures rarely satisfy the exuberant African mentality. Ritual structures that make no room for creativity, adjustment and fluidity hardly appeal to the body, soul and spirit of the Africans. For the African world view on ritual structures, limitation to *anamnesis, mimesis* and *martyria* rarely suffice. The African outgoing world view (*Weltanschauung)* includes among all else immediate and direct participation - *metasxesis. Anamnesis* demands participation - *metasxesis.*

Here the African finds himself in a kind of cross-road. An African with his boisterous background made to celebrate a ritual that seems closed to alterations, adjustments would be unfair. He is often compelled to act without conviction. This is because in the stereo-typed ritual structure he would ordinarily make adjustments, treat each case on its own merits. He would need to reshape the ritual structures to suit each case appropriately. To resort to on the spot alteration of the ritual structures would be considered disobedience to the liturgical instructions and alien to the classical Roman ritual celebration.

The aspects of *anamnesis, mimesis* and *martyria* would on the part of the assembly meet with cold response and insincerity in worship. In a most significant manner it would be next to zero participation. The African liturgical assembly becomes a peculiar one when it understands and feels at home with the ritual structure of any celebration. It abhors what the West cherishes. The West would very much appreciate a solo music accompanied by the organ for instance. For an African as long as he is familiar with the tone, the solo means nothing to him, until he could lend or add his voice even if it means only humming. The plain chant which does not allow for harmonisation would appear to the African audience or assembly as a lullaby. The assembly solves the lullaby by either harmonising the chant or join as far as he or she could.

At *(Via Crucis)* stations of the cross during Lent, the African assembly is prepared to walk on knees from one station to the next until the last station in order to imitate and share in the crude and physical sufferings of Christ. The African assembly is prepared to shed tears, bruise itself and even bleed by hard penance in imitation and participation in the sufferings of Christ. The African participant feels then that something spiritual has struck him unto achieving the goal for which he came.

Like the biblical parable of the sower, if the ritual structure fails to strike the assembly reasonably hard, there will be no root or basis for it to persevere or last even for a while. The assembly comes out of the celebration with no thrust to continuity externally. The celebration degenerates to something like a garb that is worn and pulled off hereafter with little or no reference to authentic and exemplary living afterwards. But where the ritual structures hit the African assembly, it affects and uplifts the level of participation in the secular life to a very lofty height.

During offertory for instance, where the members of the Catholic Charismatic Renewal are in attendance, the atmosphere is quite charging and electrifying thus eliciting full, active and conscious participation even if only partial. It looks like a new chapter has now opened. The structures of rituals now appear as to say: Our own chapter has now arrived, where we can show ourselves in our true and sincere worshipping form and colour.

The Exclamation: **Amen**! Response: **Amen**!;

Offering time! Response: **blessing time**!

Our Lord is good! Response: **All the time**!

All the time! Response: **Our Lord is good**!

These immediately evoke a new spirit of warmth and vibrant worship much more than what could have happened prior to this moment in celebration. This exuberance lasts until the end of the offertory when suddenly or dramatically the celebration returns to the sober, simple and stereo-typed ritual celebration that moves the assembly almost next to zero.

But where the celebrant who as a true actor displays the character of a play not himself, as earlier mentioned, he takes time to prepare the liturgy all through, then a new sense of ritual celebration definitely emerges. In effect, since the true colour of an African assembly comes to the best and maximum only during the offering time, it stands to reason that the trait should be extended to the other parts of the eucharistic celebration, namely, the greeting in the vernacular, the penitential service, the readings, the offertory time, the preface, the consecration especially at the elevations etc.

i. **Greetings**: this should be done in the vernacular.

ii. **Penitential service**: this should be done according to the cultural values and the genius of the people. The assembly is properly excited to real contrition and sorrow for the sins committed and shown the need for proper redress. The horrors of sin and its attendant consequences are skilfully mentioned. The sins of idolatry and unfaithfulness are highlighted mentioning even the local gods and deities that distract the assembly from worshipping the true God and Father of our Lord Jesus Christ. Other areas include individual sins, family sins, ills of the society, ills of the nation etc. The rite is punctuated with some appropriate local penitential hymns that prompt the assembly to true reconciliation with God, with themselves and with one another.

iii. **Readings**: To herald the liturgy of the Word, the Lectionary or the Book of the Gospels is enthroned accompanied by familiar symbolic elements like incense. It is not just throwing a few spoonful of the incense into the thurible but a pot of live charcoal with incense burning continuously as the Word is being proclaimed before the assembly. The sweet rising smoke to the heavens creates an increased sense of participation in the assembly.

iv. **Offertory dance**: This undoubtedly adds deep significant meaning and colour to the celebration.[44]

v. **Preface and other parts of the Eucharistic Prayer**: As earlier on highlighted above, immediate participation distinguishes the African approach to ritual celebration. The assembly would opt for a preface that has a refrain which gives a dialogic character to the preface. The same applies to the other parts of the eucharistic prayer. Where the celebrant does the whole thing from preface till the embolism with some interjectory refrain would not seat well in the African assembly. The need for participation- *metasxesis* comes readily into question.

x.   Structures of Rituals - Creativity in African Context

Ever before the term inculturation came into use, some remarkable progress at some inculturation had taken place in some African Churches. According to Joseph Cardinal Tomko, even if much remains to be done, certain African attitudes for instance, deep religious sense, reverence for the sacred, the way of celebrating and rejoicing in the Lord with others in a joyous, jubilant community are already incorporated into the church's liturgical life. These are all cultural aspects which edify, move and enrich the faithful of other cultures. In Africa, the Mass is truly a celebration: You Africans celebrate the Eucharist while we (the Europeans), attend or participate in it.[45] Other achievements include gestures, drums, dances, swaying, songs which are external expressions of the basic festive attitude of the African spirit. The role of the Sacred Scripture: full of imagery and narratives close to nature, is important in inculturating the faith in some places. The mysteries of the catholic faith for instance, Jesus expiatory and propitiatory sacrifice, the Eucharist are easily accepted into the African culture, the reality of sin, considered to have personal and communal forms, can also be accepted.[46]

E. E. Uzukwu in dealing with the emergent liturgies in Africa made a brief account of ways in which a united Church of Christ expressed the following of their master. This according to him led to the emergence of the various groups or families of Christians within given socio-cultural areas practising different rites. Furthermore, there emerged multiple rites in the one Church of Christ. In effect, there came about principal liturgies of the West and the East and ultimately the liturgies of Africa. The obvious result arising from this is that successful liturgical inculturation makes the christian ritual celebration a cultural experience. For instance, the rediscovery of the power of the Word of God since the reforms of the Second Vatican Council has also made a very powerful impact on Roman Catholic celebrations in Africa. Hitherto there was a very poor approach to the Word. But since after the reforms of the Council, in African Catholic celebrations the Word of God has attained a high degree of boom and boon.[47]

Furthermore, he critically examined the various directions liturgical creativity has been approached by each region. In West Africa, there are particular ways in which the eucharistic celebration is turning native among the Ashanti, Yoruba and Igbo groups. But the emerging liturgical contribution of this region to African Christianity and to the universal Church is in developing christian passage or transition rites. This region has produced a very well-developed adaptation of traditional initiation rites to the received christian rite of initiation: the *Moore ritual* in the diocese of Diebougou, Bourkina Faso; a christianisation of traditional naming ceremony (as distinct from baptism among the Yoruba and the Christianisation of Igbo (both of Nigeria) patterns of passing through crises in life with adequate rites that heal or enhance relationship (*Igba ndu*, ritual covenanting). Also in Central and East Africa afflictions by witches, evil men and women, and spirits may be resolved by participation in charismatic prayer that is widely diffused in this region. But the emergent liturgies of these areas are concentrating on the eucharistic celebration and the consecration of virgins.[48]

Some notable forms of liturgical creativity are spread across the whole continent of Africa. Actually remarkable liturgical inculturation has taken place both in the Central African Region and Eastern African Region, Francophone and Anglo-phone West African Sub-regions.

xi.   Conclusion

Dais - Base Structure System

The church stands on the dais resting on the base. The hierarchy remains on the dais and much does not take place there. Things really do happen at the base of the dais where common people like local churches are. The base level is where a lot of creativity, dreams, innovations, initiatives, dynamism and actions actually occur. The relationship between the dais few people and base people must be distinguished by mutual complementarity like what obtains in rules and creativity.

The dais people must be seen to promote and encourage the creative efforts of the base people. More powers of decision for effective implementation should be given to the heads of local churches so that things could move steadily, correctly and fast too. More of such powers would include guarding the orthodoxy of the faith which will be expressed in the ritual form of the people against the backdrop of their cultural context.

Universal Church Administration

The role of the universal administration of the church, the dais people, would concentrate more on the disciplinary rather than on dogmatic and expressive levels. As long as the essentials are kept intact, let the local heads work out and implement the expression according to their people's cultural values and genius. Like disinterested umpires in any contest, they will ensure that the rules are obeyed and skilfully implemented. Extra ordinary and more complicated issues or abuses would then require their attention for the sake of order in worship.

African Traditional Religion

The church for instance has a lot to learn from the African Traditional Religion in terms of structures of rituals for life without saying that ATR is perfect. It falls still within the competence and scope of christian evangelisation and fulfilment. The discrepancies and tensions between one ritual and another even on two similar situations do not betray the authenticity of the precious value in view. Just as there are various structures of rituals dealing with varied distressing issues in human life, one would expect the church of the third Millennium to move closer to the cultural values if not along the same line to soothe the daily human anxieties with a good listening ear and treating each case with proper ritual prescriptions on its own due merits.

In the christian dispensation, such a role is quite inevitable even today. The ability to enter into the distressing situations of people's plight and therefrom evolve a soothing and redressive ritual structure is still being cherished today.

Need for Openness

The present status of the christian structures of rituals which are eminently generalised into one for all affair would hardly be ideal and acceptable by all in their various cultures backgrounds. Without prejudice to the numerous values in the christian structures of rituals as they are hitherto, they need to do more especially in accommodating new original, more dynamic and culturally enriched structures which can stand at ease before the searchlight of the christian message.

Incidentally, this has been the clarion call of the Fathers of the reformed liturgy of the Second Vatican Council. Those who have the tendency to resist change may very soon discover to their utmost dismay to be obsolete and anachronistic. Rules and creativity exist in a mutual complementarity and thus should checkmate one another in a progressive manner. A lot have indeed been said and will continue to be said regarding the structures of rituals for life and the Africans I trust, still have a lot more to contribute as before especially in the third Millennium church that demands as a matter of urgency, a good and interested listening church.

CHAPTER TWO:

Spiritus et Sponsa – The Spirit and the Bride – A Response Towards a Practical Liturgical Spirituality for the Third Millennium Church

i.   Introduction

Commemorating the 40th Anniversary of the Constitution on the Sacred Liturgy, *Sacrosanctum Concilium*, the Holy Father, Pope John Paul II in his encyclical, *Spiritus et Sponsa*, the Spirit and the Bride, recalled that the event is a good opportunity to rediscover the basic themes of the liturgical renewal that the Council Fathers desired, to seek to evaluate their reception, as it were, and to cast a glance at the future.[49]

He further highlighted the centrality of the Paschal Mystery of Christ which needs not only to be proclaimed but also to be accomplished.[50] Sacred Music and arts have a great role to play in the liturgy of the New Millennium.[51] According to him, the liturgy of the hours ought to be celebrated with dignity.[52] Liturgy must be lived as the origin and summit of ecclesial life in accordance with the teachings of the document on the sacred liturgy, *Sacrosanctum Concilium*.

Great value should be attached to the Word of God in a manner that it meets with a positive confirmation in the celebrations. The liturgy ought to affect the practice of the faithful in a manner that it marks the rhythm of the individual communities.[53]

As a sure means of intensifying liturgical life within the communities, an appropriate formation of the pastors and of all the faithful becomes rat-her mandatory. The end in view here is to enhance active, conscious and full participation in liturgical celebrations.[54]

Liturgical studies need to be given a practical pastoral orientation for it to be meaningful especially in applying the Word to concrete human situations.[55] Great prominence ought to be given to Sunday as the day of the Lord. A Day, in which the Resurrection of Christ is especially commemorated, is at the heart of liturgical life as the foundation and nucleus of the whole liturgical year. Sunday, in a way is a synthesis of the Christian life and a condition for living the liturgical life well.[56] Liturgical celebration indeed, nourishes the spiritual life of the faithful.[57]

On the future prospects of the liturgical celebration, the Holy Father alerted the church on the various challenges which the liturgy is called to confront. We have before us a world in which the signs of the Gospel are dying out, even in regions with an ancient Christian tradition.Now is the time for New Evangelisation. According to the Holy Father, this challenge calls the Liturgy directly into question.

Spirituality seems to have been put aside by a broadly secularised society, but it is certain that despite secularisation, a renewed need for it is re-emerging in different ways in our day. This is a proof test that the thirst for God cannot be uprooted from the human heart. Therefore, some questions find an answer only in personal contact with Christ. Only in intimacy with him does every existence acquire meaning and succeed in experiencing the joy that prompted Peter to exclaim on the mountain of the Transfiguration, Master, it is well that we are here (Lk. 9:33).[58]

The Liturgy offers the deepest and most effective answer to this yearning for the encounter with God. It does so especially in the Eucharist, in which we are given to share in the sacrifice of Christ and to nourish ourselves with his Body and his Blood. However, Pastors must ensure that the sense of mystery penetrates consciences, making them rediscover the art of mystagogic catechesis. It is their duty, in particular, to promote dignified celebrations, paying the proper attention to the different categories of persons: children, young people, adults, the elderly, the disabled. They must all feel welcome at our gatherings, so that they may breathe the atmosphere of the first community of believers who devoted themselves to the Apostles' teaching and fellowship, to the breaking of bread and the prayers (Acts 2:42).[59]

Silence in worship must be fostered in our communities with greater commitment. We need silence if we are to accept in our hearts the full resonance of the voice of the HOLY and to unite our personal prayer more closely to the

Word of God and the public voice of the Church. Ours is a society filled with increasingly frenetic space, often deafened by noise and confused by the ephemeral. It is vital to rediscover the value of silence. Let us keep before our eyes the example of Jesus, who rose and went out to a lonely place and there he prayed (Mk. 1:35). We need a specific education in silence. The liturgy with its different moments and symbols, cannot ignore *silence*. [60]

The various liturgical celebrations we conduct or perform, must necessarily instil a taste for prayer, taking into account the different conditions of age and culture. Mere mechanical method of celebration is alien to traditional classical liturgy.

He challenged the pastors of souls to introduce the faithful to the celebration of the Liturgy of the Hours which as the public prayer of the Church, is a source of piety and nourishment for personal prayer. It is an action that is proper to the entire Body of the Church. Furthermore, pastors have the indispensable task of educating the faithful in prayer and more especially in promoting liturgical life, entailing a duty of discernment and guidance.

To sum up, the Holy Father, called for a Liturgical Spirituality to be developed which makes people conscious that Christ is the first liturgist who never ceases to act in the Church and in the world through the Paschal Mystery continuously celebrated, and who associates the Church with himself, in praise of the Father, in the unity of the Holy Spirit.[61] Against this backdrop, we feel challenged to make a response to this call as contained in the pages of this work.

ii.   Nature of Liturgical Spirituality

In a world replete with so many shades of spiritual experiences, a charming but challenging feeling of nostalgia for authentic spiritual experience based on the liturgy we celebrate re-echoes in the voice of the Holy Father. Liturgical experts have labored so much to clarify not only the distinctions between liturgy and spiritual life; but more importantly the mutual relationship between spirituality or spiritual life and the liturgy which the Church celebrates.

Going by the classical definition, liturgy means the public worship rendered by the mystical body of Christ in the entirety of its head (Christ) and members (the clergy and the laity) to the heavenly Father.[62] Christ in his entirety is central in the Church's liturgy. Hence the import of the word public as opposed to individual or private worship. It entails the celebration of the paschal mystery of Christ with the ultimate purpose of transforming the lives of the faithful, leading unto their sanctification, edification and glorification of God through witnessing of life. Hence the import of the word worship.

Spirituality means a consistent way of life guided by the Spirit of God. A life that is motivated, inspired and sustained by the Holy Spirit. The relationship between Liturgy and spirituality has been at the centre of attention of the liturgical renewal and is still the object of studies and research by liturgists. Both terms refer to indissociable realties of the life of the faithful and the ecclesial community. One cannot think in a consistent manner about a liturgy that does not express and nourish christian spirituality. One cannot talk about a true christian spirituality that does not find in the liturgy as celebrated and lived its source, its summit, its school.[63]

iii.   Liturgical Spirituality in Review

Liturgy was redefined by Paul VI at the very time of the approval of the liturgical constitution Sacrosanctum Concilium as the first school of our spiritual life; moreover, it is the first and most necessary source of the Christian spirit.[64] The Holy Father, went further to clarify certain key terms in his statement. The term school he explained, expresses the didactic and pedagogical character of the liturgy in its content and in its celebration: the Word of God, prayers, liturgical texts, rites and gestures, its symbolic signification, the richness of the sacraments and of the liturgical year. Through the liturgy the Church carries out daily a rich spiritual pedagogy of contents and attitudes.

The expression source indicates the mystagogical character, the initiation into the mystery, the communion with the mysteries of salvation made present in the liturgy. In this sense the liturgy is the source and summit of christian spirituality as sacramental experience.[65] Spirituality accentuates the intrinsic necessity of full participation, which welcomes and celebrates the mystery in faith, hope and love in an experience that is called to grow and mature because it is co-natural with the liturgy and with the life that follows it, the dynamism of holiness and the configuration to Christ.[66]

Christian spirituality, in its most genuine sense, must be understood as life in Christ and life in the Holy Spirit. It is existence rooted in the sacramental communion with the Lord, with his word, his life, his mysteries: thus it expresses what one calls holiness, both in its fulfilment and in its search and partial realisation in the universal call to all and in individual vocations.[67] This is the strongest sense of the christocentric vision of the life of the faithful according to Pauline and Johannine theology. It is life according to the Spirit, actuated and supported by the action of the Spirit of Christ, poured into us by means of the sacraments. Thus we come to the realisation of God's design: Christians become true children of the Father, guided by the Spirit, gathered by the Church, present in the world. The wealth of the Gospel and of the Spirit's action facilitate discussion on Christian spirituality and about various aspects of Christian life, which, in the measure that they are authentic and comprehensive syntheses of the Gospel's fundamental wealth. These are also designated by the term spirituality.[68]

The liturgical celebration, in the perspective of salvation history, marks and shapes christian spirituality with some original characteristic: the Trinitarian sense and the fullness of the aspects of the economy of salvation expressed by the Word of God and by the sacraments with all the concrete demands of life and witness. It also indicates the dynamic and progressive sense of holiness, the path of perfection for people's maturity and the growth of the reign of God. It emphasises the paschal character of christian holiness, namely the con-figuration to the mystery of Christ dead and risen, expressed initially in baptismal symbolism as a continual dying and rising.[69]

It must be noted that the Document on the Sacred Liturgy *(Sacrosantum Concilium)* supports the harmonisation of celebrating spiritually and living the celebrated mystery with two expressions of traditional liturgical spirituality: *mens concordat voci*, mind and voice should agree;[70] *vivendo teneant quod fide perceperunt*, may they uphold by their lives what they have grasped by faith.[71]

According to the Second Vatican Council, there are other extra-liturgical activities. Spiritual life is not exhausted by participation in the liturgy alone.[72]

Between the *source* and the *summit,* there exists a broad margin of the spiritual worship of life. In this margin are included all of the other activities of the faithful, without which a concrete and committed spirituality would be inconceivable. Of all these activities the Council mentions these in particular: the observance of the commandments, the works of charity, of piety, and of apostolate, the evangelisation that precedes and follows every liturgical celebration [73]; personal prayer, asceticism [74]; pious exercises. [75]

Furthermore, the liturgy is the source and summit of the spiritual life; yet it would lack something of its genuine dynamism if it were not lived with the exigencies of theological life and if it did not have a concrete influence in daily existence. The Council explicitly states: the liturgy moves the faithful, nourished by the paschal sacraments, to live in perfect union, and demands that they express in life what they have received through faith.[76] It is a demand of the dialogic dimension of salvation history to respond to God's gift, to put it into effect in actual living. Nevertheless, the importance and centrality of the liturgy in spiritual life remains. From it every undertaking of asceticism and apostolate receives light and strength; every exercise of virtue and every work of charity tend toward it.

Indeed, apostolic work is ordered so that all who have become children of God through faith and baptism might gather in assembly, praise God in Church, take part in the sacrifice and at the table of the Lord.[77] Other important activities nourished by the liturgy include: accepting and assimilating sanctification, for deepening the sense of the true worship of god, personal prayer; the nourishing of popular piety and pious exercises; the relationship between the priesthood of the believers and of spiritual worship which is recovered at a biblical, liturgical and theological level, which succeeds in tying the liturgy to the believers entire lives.[78] Thus the cultic sense of spiritual life should be applied in all its manifestations: prayer, asceticism, charity, apostolate, work, contemplation, mystical life. All is done in the dynamism of charity and in the constant action of the Holy Spirit.

In the light of this dynamism, dichotomies are overcome. The whole of Christian life, by the power of Baptism, Confirmation and the Eucharist, with the grace of the other sacraments and the practice of the virtues, becomes spiritual worship.[79]

The whole life of the faithful, every hour, day and night, is like a *leitourgia* through which they dedicate themselves in service of love to God and to humanity, joining with Christ's action who, by dwelling among us and by his self giving, has sanctified the life of all people.[80] Thus, the term *Liturgia* in the New Testament is used to designate not only the celebration of divine worship but also the proclamation of the Gospel and charity in action. In all these cases, the service of God and of humanity is involved. In liturgical celebration, the Church is a servant, in the image of its Lord, the sole *Liturgos*, since it shares in his one priesthood (*worship*) that is prophetic (*proclamation*) and royal (service of charity).[81]

In effect, between liturgy and spirituality there is a necessary dimension of continuity in life, a dynamism of interiorisation and of growth, to be and to live in Christ, to be in total conformity with the paschal mystery. The key of this unity, is the work of the Holy Spirit, whose action links celebration and life. The communion or synergy with the Spirit offers the possibility of a multiple dynamism of interiorisation and continuity: the desire and the work of the Spirit in the heart of the Church is that we live by the life of the Risen Christ. Thus the liturgy becomes the common work of the Spirit and of the Church.[82]

Every liturgical celebration should be prepared and conducted in the dynamism of the Spirit: the assembly should prepare itself for meeting the Lord, to be *people at the ready*. This preparation of the heart is the work of the Holy Spirit and of the assembly, especially of its ministers. The grace of the Holy Spirit seeks to awaken faith, conversion of heart and adherence to the Father's will. These dispositions are the conditions for accepting other graces offered in the celebration itself and for the fruits of the new life that it is intended to produce thereafter.[83]

iv. Characteristics of Liturgical Spirituality

a. Liturgical Spirituality is Trinitarian

The character of acknowledging the triune God forms the basis and sets the bearing for all other characteristics of liturgical spirituality. The Trinitarian content of liturgical spirituality underscores the primacy of Trinitarian salvific action and the gratuitous initiative and everything ultimately refers to the Trinity in an attitude where praise, thanksgiving and gratuitousness prevail. It acknowledges the Father as the source and end of every action and sets the paschal mystery of Christ in the centre with the Holy Spirit as the means of sanctification and renewal of all that is redeemed in Christ. Liturgical spirituality should mirror and effect the absolute loving unity, peace, harmony, concord, co-operation between the triune God.

The Church in her liturgy constantly invokes the Trinity in so many ways acknowledging the foundational importance of the Trinity in her life. To the Father is all prayer directed towards through the Son in the unity of the Holy Spirit.

b. Theocentric Liturgical Spirituality

Liturgical spirituality becomes theocentric when it is God centred. It acknowledges God the Father as responsible for creation of the world and its governance: *Deus est creator et rector*. He did not merely create for the sake of creating. He did not create to abandon. He creates with a divine purpose. He directs creation towards that purposeful end by his direction and governance of his creation.

c. Christocentric Liturgical Spirituality

Liturgical spirituality is Christocentric because it is Christ centred as well as deals with the celebration of the mysteries of Christ. Liturgical spirituality celebrates in the sacraments especially in the Eucharist the active and real presence of Christ who communicates his grace in its manifold richness and leads the faithful to a communion of life with him, dead and risen; in prayer and in praise it joins in his priesthood.

Liturgical spirituality underscores the (*quinque viae*) five ways in which Christ is present in the liturgy: in the gathered assembly for where two or three are gathered in my name, I am there in their midst. Christ is present in the Word, for when the Word is proclaimed he is both the proclaimed Word and the one proclaiming the Word to his mystical body, the Church. Christ is present in the minister as he performs his ministerial function vicariously of course for Christ. Christ is present in the sacraments for they are all means of encountering Christ. Christ is present in a most excellent manner in the Eucharist.[84]

d. Liturgical Spirituality is Holy Spirit Based

Liturgical spirituality recognizes the multiple activity of the Holy Spirit in the liturgy of the Church. It is the Spirit that draws the members from the four corners of the earth to form the worshipping community. Through the unction of the Holy Spirit the Church convenes to sing the praises of God and to celebrate the mystery of the Eucharist. It is the Spirit of Christ, who prays in the Church and her members.

When one does not know what prayer to offer, or to pray as one ought, the Spirit Himself intercedes for one with groans beyond all utterance.[85] It belongs to the Holy Spirit to transform the Church and her members and make her spirituality alive and meaningful. For just as the Spirit transforms the Bread and Wine into the Body and Blood of Christ, the Church prays that the same Spirit will change the members to become one body, one soul and one spirit in Christ.

Furthermore, liturgical spirituality is pneumatological because in all of its aspects of sanctification and worship, its components - Word, sacraments, signs - the Spirit of the Father and of Christ pervades the liturgy, in order to share the divine Presence with the Church and with individual believers, and fulfils in the Mystical Body the mystery of unity in one Spirit and the perfect configuration to Christ. Through Christ and in the Spirit the ultimate source and the definitive end of liturgical actions always remains the Father, whom Christ has revealed to us and whom the Spirit impels us to invoke: *Abba*, Father![86]

Again, liturgical spirituality appreciates the various gifts – charisma within her members shown in the hierarchy and liturgical ministers and functionaries. It recognises the importance of being submissive and obedient to the overseers of liturgical celebrations and their delegates or co-ordinators.[87] The acid test for these gifts are proved by the fruits which are more important than the gifts. Because fruitless gifts are as good as no gifts at all.

e. Liturgical Spirituality is Communitarian

Liturgical spirituality emphasises the Communitarian aspect of the salvific plan, the union and solidarity of all in sin and salvation, the unity of the people of God present in all legitimate local assemblies throughout the earth, the necessary communion of Saints and communion in holy things. For the spiritual viewpoint, it reaffirms the need for mutual charity in Christ and the interdependence of everyone in the common growth toward holiness.

f. Liturgical Spirituality is Ecclesial

Liturgical spirituality is ecclesial inasmuch as its expressions of worship and sanctification are regulated and established by legitimate ecclesiastical authorities. It belongs to the ecclesiastical authorities to watch over, with respect for the traditions and culture of distinct local churches, the purity and orthodoxy of the formulas and the forms of worship, and sanctification in the unity of the same apostolic faith.

g. Liturgical Spirituality is Biblical

From the point of view of constitutional elements, liturgical spirituality is biblical. The Word of God occupies an eminent place in the liturgy as an essential component of liturgical acts, inspiring the meaning of all sacraments and prayers.

The Second Vatican Council, in the Constitution on the Sacred Liturgy, expresses the great importance of the Bible in the Liturgy thus: Sacred scripture is of the greatest importance in the celebration of the liturgy. For it is from it that lessons are read and explained in the homily, and psalms are sung. It is from the scriptures that the prayers, collects and hymns draw their inspiration and their force, and that actions and signs derive their meaning. Hence in order to achieve the restoration, progress, and (adaptation) inculturation of the Sacred Liturgy it is essential to promote that sweet and living love for sacred scripture to which the venerable tradition of Eastern and Western rites gives testimony.[88]

Indeed, the liturgy is the realisation of salvation history today, proclaimed by the Word, and realised in the sacraments. The relationship between the celebration of the Paschal Mystery of Christ and the Word of God can be rightly described as very closely intimate, exclusively mutual and absolutely interdependent. The close nexus between them can be seen in terms of two moments in one act of celebration: announcement and actualisation; proclamation and action, prophecy and fulfilment, pointer and arrival; prefiguration and perfection, foretaste and fullness, expectation and realisation.[89]

The Word of God illumines the mysteries of Christ to enhance active participation in the celebration. What the Word of God announces finds fulfilment in the celebration of the mysteries of Christ. One leads to the other in such a manner that none can effectively do without the other. What the Word proclaims finds fulfilment and actualisation in the mystery that is celebrated. What the Old Testament is to the New Testament is analogously applicable to the Word and the Paschal Mystery in liturgical celebration.[90]

Against this background it could be argued that uncelebrated Word of God remains a dead word and liturgical celebration without the Word of God remains an empty celebration. The liturgical celebration consequently demands those two crucial moments of proclamation and fulfilment for meaningful celebrations of the mysteries of Christ.[91]

h. Liturgical Spirituality is Prophetic

Related to the biblical nature of liturgical spirituality is the prophetic dimension. It is a proclamation. Liturgical spirituality not only proclaims the Word of God but also proclaims the wonderful works of God, *Mirabilia Dei* in a celebrative form. Liturgical spirituality has a great deal of speaking power to even address the ills of the people and the larger society. It acts as the mouth-piece of God to his people. This is about one of the most difficult aspects of liturgical spirituality.

Without being confrontational, the prophetic nature of liturgy brings worship and the fruits therefrom face to face with people and the society.

i. Liturgical Spirituality is Mystery-Based

Liturgical spirituality is mystery-based insofar as its experience passes through the liturgical mysteries and signs; faith and catechesis help in perceiving the significance of liturgical symbols. Signs and symbols are often interchangeable in the liturgy. In the strict sense, a sign means *aliud videtur et aliud intelligitur* - one thing is seen and another is understood, e.g. smoke is a sign of fire but not fire itself; yawning is a sign of tiredness or hunger but not itself either the tiredness or the hunger. A symbol on the other hand means *quod videtur hoc intelligitur* - what is seen is understood, e. g. consecrated bread and wine are the symbol of the Body and Blood of Christ, namely the Eucharist. Both are in effect communicative although at varying degrees. Liturgical spirituality makes use of signs and symbols for communicating the mysteries of salvation through worship.

j. Liturgical Spirituality is Eucharistic

Liturgical spirituality is essentially eucharistic because it deals with the celebration of the loving sacrifice and sharing of Christ with his mystical Body, the Church. A great sense of sharing is involved in liturgical spirituality as epitomised in the Eucharist which is its main act. The concept of the Church as a communion of communities brings out much clearer the sharing element (*koinonia*) in liturgical spirituality.

The predominant theme in sharing follows the dual line of spiritual and material sharing. The former being the archetype, model and pattern for the latter. Spiritually, God shares himself in creation. He created the world to share himself, to diffuse himself for others to take part in. He then gave humanity the entire creation in a divine concessional manner so that humanity should endeavour to share with others equitably all the possessions there-in.

The Eucharist along with and at the heart of the rest of the Church's liturgical activities is at the very centre of the church's life as the activity of the church where most powerfully are achieved the sanctification of human beings in

Christ and the glorification of God,[92] and as the activity to which all other activities are directed as towards their goal.[93]

To Christ must the Church in her members demonstrate that same spiritual sacrifice of obedience to the Father's will and glorification of God and then towards fellow brothers and sisters, a gesture of liberation and sharing fairly all that is common to all after the pattern of Christ in the Eucharist: bread broken for others and blood poured out for all.

k. Liturgical Spirituality is Cyclical

Liturgical spirituality is cyclical insofar as it is marked by the temporal rhythm of the Church's celebrations without remaining imprisoned in a circle. Instead, it moves in a growing line somewhat spiral oriented toward definitive fulfilment. In different liturgical cycles (daily, weekly, yearly) with their own specific commemorative celebrations the faithful soak-deep their own existence into the mystery of Christ.

Daily prayer with the sanctification and offering of time, with its culminating point in the Eucharist, sets fleeting human time with its efforts and labour into God's salvific time and into eternity; every week the Lord's day renews, in feast and rest, the mystery of creation and of the new creation in the expectation of the Lord's definitive coming. In the yearly cycle, the faithful are placed into contact with the salvific reality of the mysteries of Christ's life and of his glorious death, to which they must conform their own lives.[94]

l. Liturgical Spiritual is Personal

Liturgical spirituality is personal while still Communitarian. The community, indeed the liturgical assembly, is made up of living persons in whom the plan of salvation is accomplished in each person with particular gifts and missions. Liturgical spirituality is as rich as it is personal, as it is personally lived and assimilated into each one's concrete circumstances in the Christian community with each ones own gifts of nature and grace (character, mentality, talents, charisma, involvement in the world). Thus liturgy realises the mystery of unity in the Spirit and in the variety of the Spirit's charisma.[95]

m. Liturgical Spirituality is Missionary

Dynamism expresses clearly the missionary dimension of liturgical spirituality. Liturgical spirituality strives to manifest the received grace to the world; after having involved the world in its intercession, the Church, which in the liturgy manifests itself as a convened community (*ekklesia*), tends to become an (*epiphania*), a manifestation of the mystery of Christ to the world by word and deed. The *leitourgia* tends toward *diakonia*, toward service of brethren in charity, toward missionary proclamation, toward dialogue.

n. Liturgical Spirituality is Eschatological

Liturgical spirituality tends towards its full realisation in glory. Sanctification and worship tend toward their perfect final expression in the heavenly Jerusalem. Every liturgical celebration, although a foretaste of the ultimate realities, is marked by hope and expectation. Every encounter with Christ in the Church refers to the hope of definitive encounter with him and the full realisation of God's reign. The liturgy arouses and celebrates the blessed hope. The liturgical texts especially the post communion prayers of eucharistic liturgy return to this expectation, which is the partially realised promise. Every celebration is a *maranatha* of the Church and of the cosmos, reaching in hope toward final consummation.[96]

o. Liturgical Spirituality is Marian

In the light of *Marialis Cultus,* liturgical spirituality is essentially Marian. The Church, in its *Marian profile*, while celebrating the mysteries makes the assembly to have the same attitudes by which the Blessed Virgin Mary associated herself with the mystery of Christ: listening and prayerful virgin, a virgin mother, a model and teacher of spiritual life for all Christians. She teaches the church to make of their own lives a worship pleasing to God.[97]

p. Liturgical Spirituality is Sanctoral

Liturgical spirituality recognises the heroism of the saints and martyrs. The church in the liturgical celebrations, presents the saints to her members to demonstrate the excellent victory of the paschal mystery of Christ.[98] The Document on the Sacred Liturgy makes this point clear when it says that by celebrating the anniversaries of saints, the Church proclaims the achievement of the paschal mystery in the saints who have suffered and have been glorified with Christ.

The feasts of the saints proclaim the wonderful works of Christ in his servants.[99] The saints are those who really followed Christ closely in his life and teachings. They serve as proven evidence of the victory of Christ in his members. Their saintliness underscores the fact that perfection as enjoined by the Lord is possible.

q. Liturgical Spirituality is Sacramental

The seven sacraments are the communications of the life of God. These sacraments are relived within the liturgical celebration. First, we must be born, that is baptism. Second, we must grow spiritually and reach the stage of christian virility, that is confirmation. Third, we must nourish our souls on the bread of life, that is the Eucharist. Fourth, we must bind up our spiritual wounds, that is penance. Fifth, we must root out all traces of spiritual infirmities, that is extreme unction. But we need government and a source of unity and the priesthood, that is the Holy Orders. And finally, we need to continue the existence of the human race, that is Matrimony.

Liturgical spirituality in its most genuine sense, must be understood as life in Christ and life in the Holy Spirit. It is existence rooted in the sacramental communion with the Lord, with his word, his life, his mysteries.

r. Liturgical Spirituality is Historical

Liturgical spirituality is historical because it appreciates the facts of history as well as the authentic interpretation of the facts of history. Liturgical spirituality develops along historical lines. It recognises historical stages of development observing positive values of history and pitfalls to be avoided. Liturgical spirituality displays an openness to various historical values and genius of various historical ages.

From the historical perspective abundant studies have been made to establish the relationship between liturgy and spirituality. In general, history contrasts the two realities that enjoyed unity at the beginning of the Church. Divergence began in the Middle Ages and became more pronounced in the *devotio moderna*. It crystallised in the Modern Era when piety and popular religiosity prevailed, and it has moved towards some harmony, not without polemics, through the years of liturgical renewal, to the Second Vatican Council, and to the present.[100] An updated history of liturgical spirituality could be important and clarifying.

s. Liturgical Spirituality is Devotional

Liturgical spirituality recognises the true and authentic devotions of the Church as means of piety and re-living the paschal mystery of Christ. For liturgical spirituality is not exhausted by participation in the liturgy alone as earlier stated (SC. 10, 12). Between the source and summit there exists pious devotions and exercises. These do not supersede the liturgy but should be patterned along the liturgical order.

Popular devotions of the christian people, provided they conform to the laws and norms of the Church, are to be highly recommended, especially where they are ordered by the Apostolic See. Devotions proper to individual churches also have a special dignity if they are undertaken by order of the bishops according to customs or books lawfully approved. But such devotions should be so drawn up that they harmonise with the liturgical seasons, accord with the sacred liturgy, are in some way derived from it, and lead the people to it, since in fact the liturgy by its very nature is far superior to any of them.[101]

t. Liturgical Spirituality is Magisterial

Liturgical spirituality recognises the importance of obedience to the teaching authority of the Church. Regulations of the liturgy depends squarely on the Church's hierarchy[102] and law of subsidiarity of the Church. Certain aspects of the liturgy are left in the hands of the Local Ordinary to regulate. Others are left to the competence of Episcopal Conferences. Others are left to the Holy See through the appropriate dicastery especially for *Recogitio*. Obedience to hierarchical order paves the way for order in worship and promotes unity in diversity as envisaged by the reformed liturgy of the Second Vatican Council.[103]

u. Liturgical Spirituality is Ecumenical and Open to Inter-Religious Dialogue

Unity of all christians and openness to other world religions form an integral part of the scope of liturgical spirituality. For, God who wills that all men be saved and come to the knowledge of the truth (1 Tim. 2:4), who in many times and various ways spoke of old to the fathers through the prophets (Heb. 1:1), when the fullness of time had come sent his Son, the Word made flesh, anointed by the Holy Spirit, to be a bodily and spiritual medicine: the Mediator between God and man. Therefore, in Christ the perfect achievement of our reconciliation came forth and the fullness of divine worship was given to us.[104]

Father may they all be one (Jn. 17:21) was the priestly prayer of Jesus. Liturgical spirituality appreciates the importance of the kind of unity which Christ intends here and intensifies her effort for the realisation of this prayer. From the text of that prayer, the unity envisaged here transcends mere unity of hearts. What is in question here appears to be an all-embracing unity: unity of everyone in everything as exemplified in the unity between the Father and his Son, Jesus Christ. The bi-nitarian unity does not allow of any distinction.

It means unity in everything. For the Church in effect, an all embracing unity entails administrative, doctrinal, liturgical, organisational and structural unity, for the Lord has earlier succinctly declared, ... there are other sheep I have that are not of this fold, and I must lead these too. They too will listen to my voice, and there will be only one flock and one shepherd. [105]

Liturgical spirituality is determined to ensure the reconciliation of all (not only Christians of other denominations and pentecostals but adherents of other major world religions: Moslems, African Traditional Religion, Hinduism, Buddhism etc.) in Christ. This prayer of Jesus could only be realised through prayer and cautious or diplomatic dialogue among the believers in Christ and other non Christian Religions.

v. Liturgical Spirituality is Ancestral

Liturgical spirituality is ancestral insofar as it recognises ancestrology in worship. Ancestrology finds inroad into the Church's liturgy on two counts: belief in the communion of the saints and the belief in the immortality of the human spirit, which is the God's consciousness in every human being (*capax Dei*).[106]

Africans for instance, believe that the ancestors whose memory still lives on in the minds of members of the society are the dead who live now a peculiar life different from the normal human existence, in the hereafter, in the great beyond. A man's spirit exists before his birth, and naturally continues after his death. It resides in his body while he is living and survives him when he is dead.[107] This is because the ancestors lived perfect and exemplary moral lives and are now interacting with living human beings through their powers. They are those persons who in their life times held key positions of importance, such as heads of families, lineage, clans, tribes, kingdoms and social groups. There are those heroes and heroines formed by the hopes of African Traditional Religion. They include those who, in various ways contributed to the expansion of well-being among their contemporaries. They are those who made life more meaningful and more worth living for their progenitors.[108]

Ancestors are not God.The cult of the ancestors in African Traditional Religion is not an idolatry. Ancestors are only venerated and not worshipped. The belief in the cult of ancestors is therefore not a negation of the faith in God even where the relationship to God is not very explicit.[109]

In relation to Christ, there may be that tendency to confuse Christology with Ancestrology. The confusion should not arise as the doctrine on each is clear enough. The ancestors do not presume to usurp the role of Christ in any way at all. Like the saints, the ancestors assume a different status to Christ. What the heroes and heroines pursued to become ancestors are found in pre-eminent, excellent and perfect manner in Christ through his incarnation and the paschal mystery. This fact is generally accepted by every culture and religion in Africa.

The idea of invoking the ancestors together with the saints has been one of the developments emerging from the recent studies on African ancestrology. Invocation of ancestors especially in the eucharistic celebration has been brought into the lime-light since the emergence of the Zairian Rite and in the Synod of Bishops, Special Assembly for Africa in Rome, April – May, 1994. Interestingly too, during the opening Mass of that synod, Pope John 11, spoke very much in favour of the African ancestors.

w. Liturgical Spirituality is Liberating and Social Justice Oriented

Liturgical spirituality is basically liberating. A meaningful celebration of liturgy must take into serious consideration the yearnings of the people and must be geared towards the liberation of the people and development of peoples. It requires making a close nexus between the liturgical celebration and social justice. The contents and the application of the fruits of liturgical celebration must go beyond the limits of the celebrative moment to overflow into and influence the various socio-politico-economic agenda that challenge the modern society.

The hitherto myopic conception of liturgy must be broadened for both the celebrants and participants to see the inestimable treasures of liberation and transformation that are co-natural with the central mysteries that the liturgy celebrates. For liturgy well celebrated and understood has the great potentiality to assess any given situation in its proper perspective, instill courage into fainting hearts, provide confidence in the midst of doubts, able to create practical options in the midst of diminishing alternatives, open up new realities and opportunities, and offering Christian courage even in the face of death. It has the power to uplift the mind to a new threshold from which it can view reality with new eyes, new hopes and new resistance.

It has the capability to transform radically and above all to make whole or holy. It would indeed be ironical if one could announce in the Eucharist that the risen Christ gives himself in food and drink for the nourishment of the world and have no concern for the millions who die for want of nourishment.

v.   Challenges Confronting Liturgical Spirituality Today

Liturgical spirituality would be relevant today if it addresses the current problems facing the world both on a global and on individual scales. Issues of social justice, racial discrimination, class distinction, globalisation, justice for women, formation of the youth in justice, massive and global unemployment, politics, economy, world order, power tussles between the first, second and third world or developing countries and poorest countries of the world, wars, political unrest, conflicts over geographical boundaries, environmental pollution, illegal population control, imbalance in international trade relations, nuclear weapons, production and proliferation of other weapons of mass destruction, the conflicting use of the Computer-Internet (today Internet which makes the world a global village, provides wide range of information and communicational data both for development and for massive destruction), insecurity, violence and terrorism, the scourge of the HIV-AIDS pandemic and more are current challenges that confront liturgical spirituality and authentic christian witnessing.

Liturgical spirituality may reach its highest form of expression in the Eucharist, but it cannot be restricted to that one liturgical exercise. There is need for further broader application of the fruits of the celebration. The use of liturgical spirituality must never be limited to the celebrating moment. Liturgical spirituality must transcend what can be found in the approved books of ritual.

vi.   Towards a Social Justice Oriented Liturgical Spirituality

Today more than ever, a direct relationship between liturgical spirituality and social justice is gradually emerging. Their mutual relationship leads the christians to experiences of transcendence. This is seen in the values affirmed in this kind of spirituality.

In recent years a more fruitful path to follow for the formation of a just liturgical spirituality has been based on the unity of the sacred and the secular. Such a perspective no longer views the world in terms of a two-storied universe. The identification of the sacred with the other-worldly and the negation of the secular is clearly rejected. It recognised that the spiritual strivings cannot denigrate the secular values that contemporary people see to be positive. God's working in the world can only be affirmed in faith, but that does not detract from the real human values in the lives of the worshipers.

The liturgy can be the privileged place for discovering the sacred within the secular. But this can only happen if we begin from the position that liturgy and life must intersect. According to Louis Bouyer, the world into which the liturgy introduces us is not a world in its own right, standing aloof, it is rather the meeting point of the world of the resurrection with this very world of ours in which we live, suffer and die.[110] The paradigm of a social justice oriented liturgical spirituality is a real human encounter that points beyond itself. [111]

vii. Conclusion

Liturgical spirituality implies involvement, engagement, commitment, participation and communion of worship and life. It deals with inspiring the extra liturgical activities with the nourishment of the liturgical celebration for a just and loving society and world at large. The dichotomy that exists between faith professed and celebrated on the one hand and the life hereafter on the other becomes a thing of the past. The transforming effects of the mysteries of Christ, celebrated in the liturgy would have to bear on the various spheres of human life without distinction.

Liturgical spirituality and social justice are tightly woven threads of the same cloth. In other words, gathering to worship and striving for social justice are not separate compartments or unrelated endeavours in the christian life, rather both are constitutive of and expression of the Church itself.

Full, conscious and active participation in the liturgy is a continuous engagement, which compels the Church, stretches her and empowers her to be full, conscious and active servant of social justice through her members. As ministers of social justice, the Church in her members must risk being broken open and transformed by the experience of the mysteries being celebrated. She must allow the ritual and the power of the liturgical celebration to shape her heart, nourish her spirit and direct her journeys.

Furthermore, there still remains an important task to be done. The task involves the formation of the youths for liturgy and justice. For the youths the relationship between liturgy and justice is of particular importance because it is a litmus test for relevancy. Youths will be inspired by the active service and authentic worship they see in lives of faith in the community. In turn, youths will inspire the community with their energy, ideas and creativity.

As members of the same mystical body of Christ ought to bridge all differences. All should be bound by the command of the Lord to love one another without distinction. The water of baptism ought to be stronger than blood relationship of kinship. For there does not exist among you Jew or Greek, slave or free, male or female. All are one in Christ Jesus (Gal. 3:28). From this mystical circle the relationship reaches out even to non believers alike.

Liturgy and life are one, seamlessly woven together by the spirit Christians learn from Christ. The Amen spoken so readily and often in the liturgy is not just an empty ritual exchange; it is a commitment to be carried out in life as well. It has to be well noted finally that liturgy is neither the problem nor the solution. Full and active participation in the liturgy is not a panacea for the world's ills, or even the Church's. Liturgical spirituality must lead to making a difference in people's lives, calling them into community, deepening their sense of prayerful worship and creating new spiritual awareness.

CHAPTER THREE:

Ite Missa Est - Go the Mass is Ended: Implications for Missionary Activities in the Third Millennium Church

i.   Introduction

Very much like a drop of honey which attracts so many bees, the eucharistic celebration draws together various people of various ranks in the society. Who could be missing at a typical parish Sunday eucharistic liturgy? Indeed, the celebration includes everyone who could come in. Everyone is invited to participate although in varying degrees. This very well obtains both in the urban and suburban areas. Christ brings all people together for worship so that at the end they like the apostles and the disciples could be sent out on mission. The wide variety of people who take part in the celebration thus are mandated to explore possibilities of penetrating their various worlds with Christ and his message of joy, hope and salvation.

Ite Missa est remains a positive command. It excludes any tendency towards inertia. It challenges all participants to stand up and act for Christ in the world around oneself. It does not mean go until we meet again without any practical undertaking. It does not simply mean go, we shall see again. It does not mean go, and continue business as usual. It does not mean go and rest. It rather means go, react and act; go, imitate what Christ did and continue from where he stopped. It means go and evangelise; go and light up other candles of hope in the world; go and wake the sleeping giants; go and become bread broken for others; go and be sacrificed for others; go and re-enact the sacrament in a practical manner; go and form the body of Christ from the body of Christ which was received during the celebration; go and become apostles with unlimited scope; go and become disciples intent on winning souls for him and revolutionise the world with the power of Christ; go and fight on the side of Christ and with the armour of Christ; go and become the mouth-piece of Christ; go and infuse the world values with the transforming values of Christ; go and restore Christendom in the world.

At the end of the eucharistic celebration, the assembly is dismissed with these thoughtful and purposeful injunctions: Go, go into the world to make the world holy. May the sacred banquet you have celebrated inspire and motivate you to sanctify the world around you. What you have celebrated calls for dynamism and evangelisation. It demands action not complacency. Share the light of the celebration with others and go about bearing witness to the mystery you have celebrated. *Ite Missa est* means unequivocally that the assembly is sent. This mandate is continuously renewed in the assembly as often as the assembly attends the eucharistic worship.

As a parting farewell, *Ite missa est* sends the Church forth to continue the work of Christ in the world. The mandate calls for missionary activities in the world. The command makes a great shift of understanding of the Eucharist from purely individualistic, private and one sided approach that aims merely at the salvation of souls. The command instead opens up a wider horizon of eucharistic concept to include the salvation of the temporal order which is basic for the salvation of souls. It broadens the scope of the eucharistic celebration to reach out to the salvation of the entire created order, the soul as well as the spirit and body, the social, the economic, the political, the environment, inter personal and international relationships.

If bread and wine, fruits of the earth and the work of human hands could metamorphose and bring into reality the presence of Christ, so much so would they transform the entire creation by bringing the presence of Christ to all the nooks and crannies of the world order. Bread and wine eventually become a small index of a big whole. The Eucharist becomes therefore the sacrament of global transformation through the dynamic instrumentality of the worshipping community.

ii.   Evolution of the Term *Missa*

The translation of the word *Missa* with Mass was the result of a rather long and complex evolution which ended at about the end of the fifth and the beginning of the sixth century, when the term Mass was applied to the entire eucharistic celebration. The first century christians preferred to designate the

Mass with such terms as *Fractio panis* - breaking of bread, *Eucharistia* - Eucharist, *Oblatio* - offering and other such terms.[112]

Originally, the word *Missa,* indicates the dismissal at the end of every meeting or assembly, but it was rarely used in the context of the eucharistic celebration. In the course of time, the meaning of the word began to assume a wider connotation. It passed from the simple meaning of dismissal at the end of an ordinary reunion or meeting to assume the totality of the orations that conclude a celebration.[113] For the monks, *Missa* stands for the group of final prayers of the divine office.[114] Later on, *Missa* stood for the entire divine office, and this provoked between the end of the fifth century and the beginning of the sixth century, the habit of associating the term *Missa* with the combined liturgy of the Word and the Eucharist.[115] There are thus, three stages of development of the term *Missa* as follow:

i.   dismissal and final prayer of a celebration

ii. entire celebration of the divine office

iii. the entire eucharistic celebration.

The translation of *Missa est* with the Mass is ended looks like a contradiction in terms and again, one has to speak of *Missa* with the understanding of sending praise to the Father. If *mittere* means to send, or re send, to return or send back, let go or leave to go, to translate *Ite Missa est*, giving it here the meaning of a mission entrusted to those who have participated in the Eucharist is an expression called pastoral, which does not have corroboration in the reality of the text. The poverty of this term to designate that which constitutes the centre of christian life (the Eucharist) was being made known by the Fathers of the Church like St. Gregory the Great, who was so passionate with the expression *Missarum Solemnia* - Solemn Mass (for the Eucharist as a technical term) and Cesarius of Arles who used freely the expression *Sacra Mysteria* - sacred mysteries (for the Eucharist also as a technical term).

iii.   *Missa* as Dismissal in the East and West (non Roman)

Just as at the close of fore-Mass,[116] once the prayer of blessing had been said over those who were told to leave, there follows a formal dismissal. So it was most probable that there was always such a dismissal also at the end of the entire service. One cannot expect much more than the word with which the one presiding at every well-ordered assembly ordinarily announces the close, especially when the farewell blessing has just preceded. Such announcement of the conclusion was common in ancient culture, at times even using the word *missa*.

In the strict christian usage, the corresponding formula often acquired a religious or a biblical signification. In the East, John Chrysostom witnessed to the use of the formula of dismissal in Antioch and Egypt in the cry of the deacon:

poreuesthe en eirene - Go in peace.

This greeting has remained customary especially in Egypt.

In Byzantium, the greeting says:

En eirene proelthomen - Let us go in peace.

Similarly, in both East and West Syria, the greeting acquired a much stronger religious tone:

En eirene Christou poreuthomen - Let us go in the peace of Christ.

In all the Eastern (Greek) liturgies the cry is followed by the answer of the people: *En onomati kuriou* - In the name of the Lord.[117]

In the West, that was also the formula used in the Church of Milan.[118] Here, the invitation to leave reads:

Procedamus cum pace - Let us proceed with/in peace! is answered by saying:

In nomine Christi - In the name of Christ.

A longer formula, which indicates the ending of the service only retrospectively, is found in the Mozarabic Mass:

Sollemnia completa sunt in nomine Domini nostri Jesu Christi - the celebrations are ended in the name of our Lord Jesus Christ.

Votum nostrum sit acceptum cum pace - May our sacrifice or offering be accepted with peace or in peace.

The people responded: *Deo gratias* - Thanks be to God.

iv. Dismissal Formula in the Earlier Roman Historical Setting

The formula *Ite Missa est*, in contrast with all the aforementioned appears very laconic. But this is typical of the essential genius of the Roman liturgy. In Rome people had a realistic and practical spirit. They used a formula of juridical character: *Ite, Missa est* - Go, the Mass is ended.

Missa from *mittere* (Latin) to send as mentioned above, means dismissal. Later on at about fourth century forward *Missa* came to designate the liturgical action which preceded, that is the Mass.[119]

The formula *Ite Missa est* must have been so widely used with this meaning that it became in particular a technical expression for the conclusion of eucharistic assembly, otherwise, a phrase like *finis est* would rather have been employed. The formula had this meaning at least as far back as the fourth century, while on the other hand, this meaning was no longer current in the early Middle Ages. So even the first literary evidence for the *Ite Missa est* is found in the Roman *ordines*, and so one would not be blundering if one held that this formula was as old as the Latin Mass itself.[120]

A corroborating argument is found in the fact that similar formulas were prevalent in the everyday social life of the Romans. After a funeral for instance, the assembled mourners were dismissed with the word *Ilicet* which is the same as *Ire licet* - be free to go.[121]

According to the bronze tablets of *Iguvium*[122] from the last century before Christ, the conjoined blessing of the people and cursing of the strangers closed with the cry: *Itote Iguvini - Go citizens of Iguvium*. There were other formulas stipulated for the conclusion of gatherings in political life.

v. Dismissal Formula In The Gallican Liturgy

Benedicamus Domino - Let us bless the Lord could have been a concluding formula of the Gallican liturgy. For although there are apparently no signs of it in Roman sources before the year 1000, there are traces of it considerably earlier in Frankish territory. The *Ordo Angilberti - Ordo of Angilbert* of about the year 800, in describing the order of Communion on high festivals, mentions that after the *completio missae* - completion of the Mass, the people left (*laudantes Deum et benedicents Dominum*) praising God and blessing the Lord. In an *Ordo* for the sick from about the same time, one finds that after the giving of Communion: *Tunc data oratione in fine dicat sacerdos: Benedicamus Domino. Et respondeant omnes, Deo gratias, et expletum est* - Then having given the prayer at the end the priest says: Let us bless the Lord. And all respond, Thanks be to God and it is completed.

In the eleventh century, however, an adjustment was made between these two formulas, such as we have at present: the *Ite missa est* is used whenever there is a *Gloria*; the: *Benedicamus domino* is used on the other days without *Gloria*. But efforts were made to find a deeper reason for this merely outward division. The days with *Ite missa est* are days of a festive character, when the entire populace is assembled, so that the invitation to leave at the end of service has a meaning, while the days with *Benedicamus Domino* are days when only the *religiosi* - the religious, the pious whose life is more especially devoted to spiritual service, are present; whereby the priest, without turning around, urges them, and himself with them, to continue praising God.

Later on, the use of the two formulas became interchangeable. The *Benedicamus domino* was as much a formula of departure for the assembled faithful as the *Ite Missa est*. Here both received the same response of *Deo gratias*. Then the response was given a religious tone just as the acknowledgement of the message receives a religious expression in the *Deo gratias*. However, one must admit that when the lines were drawn for the use of the two formulas, considerations like those referred to above, especially the solemn character of certain festivals, played a part. Also when the divine service was continued, as at the midnight Mass of Christmas, when Lauds followed, or on Maundy Thursday and the vigils of Easter and Pentecost, preference was given to the invitation to praise God, *Benedicamus domino*.

Again, since the *Ite missa est* was considered an expression of joy, it had to disappear from the Requiem Mass. So one discovers that since the twelfth century the *Requiescant in pace* begins to supplant it.

When the herald in olden times announced the conclusion of an assembly, he did so with a corresponding raising of his voice. The judge, the official of the state, remembering his dignity, speaks in a moderate tone, but the herald lets his cry resound loudly over the whole assembly. It could not be much different in the case of a dismissal from divine service.

As a further step, the *Ite missa est* must soon have been provided with a special singing tone. Already in the tenth century there must have been various melodies which were richly adorned with *melismas*; for this time also marks the appearance of tropes, the expanding texts which set a syllable to each note of the melody. On the other hand, there seem to have been no tropes for the *Benedicamus domino* in the Mass.

The *Ite missa est* has kept another sensible expression of its function as a call to the people: just like the greetings, it is pronounced with face turned to the people. Hence this cry has always remained a manifest closing point of the service.

vi.   Dismissal Formula in the Recent Roman Rite

As mentioned above, in Rome *Ite Missa est* means quite simply: *Go, this is the dismissal*, as if one were saying: *Go it is finished* or more seriously, *Go, the meeting is concluded.*[123] *Ite missa est* was originally at every Mass, no matter what its character was [124] and probably at the end of other services. The dismissal is the formal conclusion of the liturgical assembly. If another liturgical function is to follow immediately the dismissal is omitted.

It is the deacon's responsibility in the Roman Rite to dismiss the liturgical assembly. In the absence of a deacon, the presiding presbyter offers the dismissal to which the assembly responds: *Deo gratias* - Thanks be to God.

Like the liturgical greetings, normally in vernacular celebration the dismissal would be recited or chanted. However solemn seasons could be emphasised by the chanting of the dismissal formula, especially during Eastertide when *Alleluia* could be appended to both the dismissal and its response.

The formula *Ite missa est* signified that the liturgical gathering was concluded and the people were free to go. Many modern translations supplement the juridical formula with missionary themes: e.g.,

i.   *Go in peace to love and serve the Lord.* Response: Thanks be to God.

ii. The French Missal was inspired by the formula of Eastern Syria: *Go in the peace of Christ.* Response: Thanks be to God.

iii. The English Missal does the same. It unites the East with Rome by proposing further: The Mass is ended. Go in peace. Thanks be to God.

iv. Finally it adds a third, very beautiful formula: Go in peace to love and serve the Lord as given above too. Response: Thanks be to God.

v.   The German Missal appears very laconic like the Roman: *Geht hin in Frieden - Go in peace. Dank sei Gott dem Herrn* - Thanks be to God.

vi. The Italian Missal resumes the elaborate formula:

La Messa e finita, andiamo in pace - The Mass is ended Let us go in peace.

Response: *Rendiamo grazie a Dio* - Thanks be to God.

vii. The Igbo (Nigerian) Missal says:

Missa agwusigo, nabanu n'udo - The Mass is ended, go in peace.

Response: *Ekene diri Chukwu* - Thanks be to God!

vii.   Dismissal Formula in Review

a. Go the Mass is ended! or Go in the peace of Christ!

New era of Evangelisation acknowledges the primary role of the Eucharist. The role of the Eucharist in the new era of evangelisation cannot be over stressed. As a method in theology and inculturation, evangelisation relies very much on the Eucharist. It is its raison d'être. It is indeed, the *source* and *summit* of effective evangelisation.

First there is an impression. The impression emanates from the fact that such formulas that say, Go the Mass is ended, or Go in the peace of Christ look very much opposed to the theme of the discussion. They seem to have no missionary connotation. They appear to be self enclosed with no sense of sharing all that one has experienced and encountered during the liturgical celebration with others. Such spiritual encounter and experience ought to remain with self or group. These simply display a kind of self directed spirituality with no sense of passing on the peace of Christ or the encounter one had during the bounteous banquet with Christ to others. This could lead to eucharistic minimalism.

Eucharistic minimalism sets in when an aspect of the celebration fails to bring out the full import of what it is meant to convey. Self directional restriction of the dismissal formula would rather be a kind of one-way- traffic spirituality which is foreign to the classical traits of the Roman liturgy. The dynamism and challenge of the assembly at the end of the eucharistic celebration seem to be diminished if not entirely lost when the people are dismissed by such laconic formulas.

b. Go in Peace to Love and Serve the Lord!

The dismissal of the eucharistic worshipping community with the formula, Go in peace to love and serve the Lord, gives the closest approximation to the missionary mandate of the discussion. The formula obviously transcends the self-exclusive eucharistic spirituality, the one directional scope of the eucharistic effects, and the static dimension of the Eucharist. The formula has a clear thrust and vision to missionary and evangelising activities. The worshipping community has been well equipped with the peace of Christ which is meant to be diffused (*dapper tutto a tutti ovunque dispersi*) everywhere to everyone where ever they may be.

In point of fact, within the eucharistic celebration the mysteries of Christ with all its saving powers, transformative capacity, sanctifying effects, edifying orientation and God glorifying tendencies are easily made available to the worshipping assembly. The members of the worshipping body are sufficiently equipped with the liberating energies of Christ from all forms of slavery especially of sin and death as a paradigm for other forms of liberation in the world around and in the larger society. The assembly is made to feel the pulse of one another, a feeling that ought to be extended to others outside the assembly as a post celebration activity.

The double encounter involved in effective missionary activity emanating from the eucharistic celebration demands further clarification. There has to be first and foremost, the first encounter with the Lord himself which gives rise to information, formation, learning, education, experience, encounter, transformation, sanctification, edification and God glorification of the worshipping assembly during the course of the eucharistic celebration.

The second encounter that completes the oscillation of the missionary pendulum involves the post celebration activity of disseminating, extending, sharing the eucharistic values by engaging, involving, participating in and influencing the world with the christian values through witnessing. The second has no meaning without the first and the first has no relevance without the second. In such double encounter lies the effectiveness of the eucharistic missionary mandate of *Ite missa est*, Go, in peace to love and serve the Lord.

c. Christ and Missionary Mandate

Christ very much believed in the importance of the double encounter for effective missionary work. What was the first command of Christ to his apostles? Come! Come! Come! Come and see.[125] The apostles came, saw, encountered, remained and experienced the Lord such that they were reluctant even to leave. But they had to leave to pass on the message to others. That brings one to the second encounter of doing effective missionary work.

What was the last command of Jesus to his apostles before he ascended to the Father? Go! Go! Go! Go and make disciples of all nations.[126] One could correctly imagine that the eucharistic command is very much patterned in a similar way. First come, come, come for the encounter with the eucharistic Lord and later on, go, go, go[127] and certainly not to go and rest or relax but work.[128]

The come - go double encounter even took place before his final departure from the apostles. The two accounts of the missionary journeys in Luke's gospel describe the come - go encounter very succinctly.

d. Gospel of Luke: 9:1-10; 10:1-12

These two instances from Luke's gospel describe the missionary journeys made by the twelve apostles and the second made by the seventy disciples of Christ in Lk. 9:1-9 and 10: 1 -12 respectively. In each case, Christ sent them. There are other parallels of these accounts in the other synoptics. The choice of Luke's version is as a result of its special relevance to the topic under discussion.

Missionaries are like emissaries of the king. They are very much like ambassadors. They carry the message of the king as well as the image of the country they represent wherever they go.

In sending the apostles and the disciples respectively, Christ took the initiative. In either case, they were appointed by Christ and not elected by the people. They were to represent no other, than Christ and carry his message and image to the people.They were chosen by Christ and not campaigned for by the people. They were selected by Christ and not sponsored by anyone for the mission. The first missionary account was restricted to the twelve with restricted area of jurisdiction. The second missionary account by the seventy disciples had a larger group with wider geographical area to cover. As God sent Christ in the Incarnation[129] with full power and authority so also Christ sent his apostles and disciples respectively with power and authority over the devil, unclean spirit, curing all diseases and to preach the kingdom of God.

Today, the same Christ at the end of the eucharistic meal in a still much larger scale sends the Church to do exactly the same work as their predecessors to the larger society of the entire world. For instance in checkmating political aspirants, their manifestos and promises to the masses with the search light of the Word as proclaimed in Mtt. 25:31-46.[130]

The first missionary account by the apostles has something very significant both then and today. The account over and over again, joins *preaching* and *healing: heal the sick and preach the kingdom.* This is very important in today's missionary work. The dichotomy which some missionaries often make today by emphasising the preaching over the healing or vice versa is not biblical. Missionaries are meant to join concerns for people's bodies and their souls.

The message of Christ must be seen in its wholistic perspective. It should not be seen only in words, however comforting; but also in deeds. It was a message which was not confined to news of eternity; it was meant to change conditions on earth. It was the reverse of a religion of *pie in the sky*. Christ's message to the missionaries insisted that health to people's bodies was as integral a part of God's purpose as health to their souls. Nothing has done the Church more harm than the isolation of one of these from the other.[131]

It is possible of course to over-stress material things. But it is equally possible to neglect them. The Church will forget only at her peril that Jesus first sent out his men to preach the kingdom and to heal, to save people in body and in soul.[132]

The first command as earlier highlighted is purposeful. An invitation is given to be catechised, discipled, apostled, taught, feasted, nourished, groomed and fashioned after the image of the Host. Hereafter, the command assumes a missionary dimension *Ite, Go, Geht, Andiamo,* etc. Go and do likewise to others you meet anywhere at any time.

The package contained in the missionary command covers a great deal. It includes *go* and *evangelise* the world around. *Go* and *proclaim* the Good news. What is proclaimed must be *good* and must be *news.* It must not degenerate to something bad and stale. Go and declare the *Mirabilia Dei* - the wonderful works of God in salvation history as one has rightly experienced and encountered in the eucharistic celebration.

Go and make Christ *known*, make him *present* in the life of everyone and make him *loveable.* Go and conquer the world with the loving spirit of Christ. Educate the world from the perils of error and ignorance. Teach the world the truth of life in Christ. Preach the Word of God in season and out of season, accepted or unaccepted. Insist on it. Shatter the stubbornness and the unbelief of the people with the power of the Word of God. Feed and nourish the famished world with the life giving bread of life against the background of the multiple spiritual junk food that besiege the world's table.

It includes furthermore, the total transformation of the world with the good and revolutionary loving message of Christ. Reconcile and build bridges of love among the warring sections of the populace on all levels. Instil into the socio-political spheres the values of Christ especially with regard to humane and benign administration as well as mounting programmes that are development of the peoples oriented. Justice, peace and love are the raw materials as well as the basis for the progress of the people. Sanctify the world through authentic christian witnessing.

viii. *Ite Missa Est* - Implications for Missionary Activities Today

The dismissal formula, Go in peace to love and serve the Lord encapsulates the entire missionary dimension of the Eucharistic celebration. Apart from the spiritual growth, the formula calls for socio-economic and political transformation through the eucharistic mystery that has been celebrated. In other words, the relevance of the eucharistic celebration on the social dimension of the larger society as the Eucharist transcends the mere salvation of the soul to include the dynamic outward sign of how life should be shared and lived after celebration. A number of implications flow from this.

a. *Ite Missa Est* Mitigates the Extremities of Liturgists and Social Activists

For some time now, liturgists are turned off by the social activists and their objectives because the social activists appear to have no interests in, or respect for, the canons of authentic liturgy. On the other hand, social justice activists write off liturgists and liturgy because the liturgists seem unconcerned that their liturgy may be reinforcing an unjust *status quo*.

In the midst of mutual suspicion against these important but uncoordinated interest groups, a concerted effort to overcome the split becomes obvious. Liturgical renewal and reform are impossible in isolation from efforts to restructure the social order. Social justice ministry without renewed worship on the other hand lacks roots and cannot achieve its goal.[133]

b. *Ite Missa Est* Awakens the Consciousness of Liturgy and Social Justice

A glaring aspect of relating the liturgy that is celebrated and life is the evolution of a liturgy that is justice oriented. A liturgy that incarnates injustice in its very structures becomes a liturgy that is unjust. The same applies to a liturgy which has intercessory prayers which deal with economic and political tensions, but which continues to employ the kind of imagery and language which sets up a sacred - secular dichotomy in world view and spirituality. A liturgy that is justice oriented excludes such a liturgy which has a sermon on what may

81

be the prevailing social concerns, but which continues to operate according to an institutional model of liturgical understanding that improves nothing practically.[134]

To be sent out with the mandate *Ite missa est*, impels the worshippers to strive for social justice which they have experienced in the celebration. The liturgical experience they have had must possess qualities of justice which have to be exercised outside of worship.

Against this backdrop, liturgy becomes a form of ritual, that means a patterned symbolic activity, which must be permeated by a way of thing, a way of acting, and way of relating where individual worth, fairness, rights, and responsibilities are recognised and promoted. Worshippers who engage in this bundle of symbols called liturgy must find themselves within an open-ended situation where they have the opportunity and room to experience justice among themselves and justice within themselves.[135]

They must be able to experience a sense of the wholeness of human life in terms of the rite which ultimately speaks of the Paschal Mystery. Through their continual participation they know on all levels, not just the intellectual, what human justice is. A liturgy that does justice certainly makes it easier for people to recognise what forms justice should take in any concrete situation outside of worship. But it does not do this by becoming a recipe book for people working on international issues, or in the inner city, or in the various areas of gender oppression. Rather it does this by creating the possibility for worshippers to have a justice experience which they can then use as a norm or measure to judge what would be and are the authentic experiences of justice in the rest of life.[136]

We cannot know what to do justice-wise simply through analytical study or hortatory instruction. It is important to have other analogous experiences of justice before we can recognise injustice and can facilitate programs for justice.[137]

c. *Ite Missa Est* Connects Eucharistic Liturgy with the World of Work

The United States Roman Catholic Bishops in their pastoral letter in 1986, challenged the US economic life with the christian vision. They maintained that economic life and christian vision calls for a deeper awareness of the integral connection between worship and the world of work. Worship and common prayers are the wellsprings that give life to any reflection on economic problems and that continually call the participants to greater fidelity to discipleship. To worship and pray to God of the universe is to acknowledge that the healing love of God extends to all persons and to every part of existence, including work, leisure, money, economic and political power and their use, and to all those practical policies that either lead to justice or impede it. Therefore, when christians come together in prayer, they make a commitment to carry God's love into all these areas of life.[138]

The unity of work and worship finds expression in a unique way in the Euch-arist. As people of a new covenant, the faithful hear God's challenging word proclaimed to them. The word gives a message of hope to the poor and oppressed and they call upon the Holy Spirit to unite all into one body of Christ. For the Eucharist to be a living promise of the fullness of God's King-dom, the faithful must commit themselves to living as redeemed people with the same care and love for all people that Jesus showed. The body of Christ which worshippers receive in Communion is also a reminder of the reconciling power of his death on the Cross. It empowers them to work, to heal the bro-kenness of society and human relationships and to grow in a spirit of self-giving for others.[139]

The liturgy teaches the assembly to have grateful hearts: to thank God for the gift of life, the gift of this earth, and gift of all people. It turns hearts from self-seeking to a spirituality that sees the signs of true discipleship in the sharing of goods and working for justice. By uniting the assembly in prayer with all the people of God, with the rich and the poor, with those near and dear and with those in distant lands, liturgy challenges the members to a way of living and refines their values. Together in the community of worship, members are encouraged to use the good of this earth for the benefit of all. In worship and in deeds for justice, the Church becomes a sacrament, a visible sign of that unity in justice and peace that God wills for the whole of humanity.[140]

d. *Ite Missa Est* Makes Liturgy a Non Private - Affair

Liturgy by simple definition is a public worship as earlier on well indicated. Liturgy whose main component is the eucharistic celebration, is not a private or individual affair. It incorporates both the individual and the worshipping community whose influence are experienced outside the worshipping community and to the larger society. Eucharistic liturgy underscores social dimension of the worshipping community challenging them to influence the world around them with the revolutionary social values they have imbibed as they worshipped. Invariably, a number of factors in the culture could prevent one from hearing the liturgy's message with regard to social justice.

A prominent factor is the assumption that religion and therefore worship are private affairs with nothing to say about organising society. It is recognised, of course, that religion and liturgy can support the social order by helping citizens endure the sometimes unpleasant features of society, or it can threaten the social order by raising citizens' expectations. From the social environment, Christians absorb this mentality of religion as a private affair. When people assemble for liturgy, they least expect that it will have anything to say to them about their changing the structures of life in the society to bring about social justice. They do not hear any such message even when, from time to time, the liturgy speaks it more explicitly. They are surprised, perhaps even offended, when preachers challenge the public life of their city, state, or nation, the government or business or criminal justice or public education. Preachers are thought to be out of order in bringing up such subjects.[141]

Secondly, it is also assumed that what worship has to say for the private welfare of the worshipping assembly has nothing to do with society's structures. Worship has little to do with worldly existence other than enable the assembly to bear its trials in view of promised happiness after this life. The liturgy is essentially about that promised happiness in another world, so they do not expect the liturgy to speak about the present social order, except to encourage people to accept, in the spirit of Christ, the sufferings the social order may impose upon them.[142]

Furthermore, many do not hear the liturgy's message of social justice, because they do not need to hear it for themselves and so they do not hear it for others either. They feel that they are not suffering any great injustice, at least they are not conscious of such suffering. Economically they live respectably and are able to fulfil some of their desires. They complain about taxes, waste in government, high food prices, extreme costs of medical care, the fuel hike, but they do not experience themselves being reduced to helplessness. As members of the upper and middle classes, they are not likely to hear the social justice message in the liturgy because their particular needs do not attune them to that meaning of their worship. Only if, somehow, they can acquire a sense of solidarity with the truly unjustly deprived people of their city, state, nation, and world, will they discern the call to action for social justice in liturgical celebrations.

Or they may discover that they are indeed oppressed people suffering injustice, even though it may not be as obvious as the injustice suffered by the economically impoverished, the politically disenfranchised, the socially segregated, or the culturally deprived.[143]

e. *Ite Missa Est* Confirms Liturgy as Social Justice Oriented

Eucharistic liturgy indeed, refers much more to social justice than most people suspected. Incidentally, not many if any at all detect that meaning or been moved to concern themselves about injustice in the society as a result of their liturgical participation.

One possible reason for this failure on the part of the liturgical participants to experience the social justice dimension in the liturgy, could be that the society conditions people, so that they do not discern the liturgy's message of social justice. People's minds and hearts, their perspectives on life, their attitudes and values are shaped by their culture. When people come to celebrate the liturgy, they are simply not looking for the truths and values in the realm of justice which are contained there. They often come in and wait to be dismissed with *ite missa est* only to continue their daily business as usual. They miss the mandate of Christ, for instance when he said, in Luke, *go and do the same in the case of the good Samaritan,* or when Jesus concluded the parable of the seed with the exhortation, *let the one who has ears to hear me, hear.*

ix. Social Justice in the Liturgy of the Eucharist

The celebration of the Eucharist has very many implications for social justice. The Eucharist by nature unites the church intimately with risen Lord who sacrificed himself for the Church and the world, who emptied himself, *kinosis* in Greek, self-emptying, Philippians 2:6ff, taking the form of a slave for human liberation from slavery, and who, though he was rich, became poor, so that we who are poor might become rich. Every Eucharistic celebration unites us to that same Lord Jesus and has innumerable implications for social Justice.

a. Nature of Social Justice

People naturally, live in community. They come together as individuals to form a family. Families come together to form a neighbourhood. Several neighbourhoods come together to form a city; several cities come together to form a nation. The eventual union of all nations will form a global society. As individuals, however, people have rights which stem from their gift of life: they have a natural right to the means to sustain life, and they have a natural right to make their lives what they were intended to be.

As individuals in society, people have rights to those things in society which will enable them to sustain life and make life what it was intended to be in the society. These rights inevitably mean responsibilities in the society, responsibilities which insure that everyone's rights in the society will be safeguarded within the limitations inherent in societal living. The safeguarding of the individual rights within the limitations of societal living is what social justice is all about. Social justice is based on people's God-given rights not only to the means to sustain life, but also to the means to achieve the quality of life intended by God.

If people lived alone, in isolation from each other, there world be no need for social justice. But the fact that they do live in society, creating a whole chain of interrelated associations, makes a special kind of justice necessary, namely, social justice. Social justice is necessary to make society work, for it governs people's relations with each other in society. It encompasses whatever is right and fitting in people's relationships with each other in social living, including not only laws that insure people's rights, but the common amenities and courtesies which make living in society gracious. With social justice civilisation progresses; without it, there would be no civilisation at all.[144]

As we joyfully journey together with James L. Empereur and Christopher G. Kiesling, through the various parts of the eucharistic celebration, we shall discover a lot of social justice implications therein.

b.   The Gathering Assembly for Eucharistic Worship

As the assembly gathers from their various homes in the neighbourhood, they are meant to be prompted to think of the housing needs of the poor and elderly and calls to mind discriminating practices in renting by inhuman landlord and selling of property. As a result, the very need to assemble for the Eucharist is a reminder that people are social beings, they are called to justice for only in loving justice can people live socially in a way commensurate to the dignity of each one.[145]

Right there in the church one sees all sorts of people: rich and poor, healthy and disabled, young and old, business executives and employees, office workers and factory owners. The only distinctions that can be made in the eucharistic assembly are those arising from liturgical functions or due occasionally to civil authorities in accord with the liturgical law. In this worshipping assembly, one discerns the basic equality and dignity of every person vis-a vis God and therefore, the rights of every person to a fair share of the earth's and society's resources which are God's gifts for all her children.[146]

c.   The Procession and Entrance Hymn

At the beginning of the celebration, the presider and the other ministers process down the central aisle from the rear of the church. The participants in that procession should remind the assembly of social justice by displaying a retinue of female and male ministers. Even the hymn that accompanies the procession rules out gender language for instance perpetuating masculine terms like brother, man, mankind, he, his him in a generic sense, when the large portions of the population do not interpret them in that way and are offended by them and when no conceivable harm can come to those who still accept them in an inclusive sense.[147] Furthermore in preaching, however, and eventually in liturgical texts, conscientious efforts can and should be made to balance the masculine names with feminine terms found in scripture and also meant to tell us something about God.

d.   General Intercessions

The faithful intercede for the church, civil authorities, the salvation of all, and those oppressed by various needs. The General intercessions are meant to broaden the vision of the local assembly, to lift the gathered people beyond their own immediate problems, worries and needs to make them conscious of all God's children scattered far wide over this planet, millions of which are suffering from hunger, malnutrition, ignorance, homelessness, political imprisonment, torture etc.

e.   The Offertory - Bringing on of Gifts

At the presentation of gifts more than one person leave their places in the pews to pick up the gifts: bread, water, wine and then process with them down the aisle to the ministers in the sanctuary. Here the gathered assembly who celebrate the death, resurrection and future coming of Jesus Christ bring those gifts to the table. Those people are the representatives of the assembly carrying those gifts to the table. Some key questions are inevitable here. What are being carried to the sanctuary? The fruits of the earth and the vine which are God's gift to all of God's creation. In the offertory, the church brings to God the beauty and bounty of his creation. These are the golden fields of wheat and fat clusters of grapes.

Furthermore, the assembly brings to the table more than the fruits of the earth. It brings the work of human hands. It brings the product of human effort, indeed, social effort. It offers the entire world to God. But as it offers the entire world to God, can it fail to be concerned about the social injustice that corrupts that same world, that taints the gift. At the price of what oppression does the assembly carry up to the table gifts of bread and wine. Who has been hurt in the long process in which that bread and wine have made their way from the fields and the vines? Migrant workers and their children.

Does the assembly dare to offer God mouldy bread and sour wine. Mouldy and sour not because of some bacteria, but because of the social injustice suffered by so many of the men, women and children through whose efforts this and wine come to be here in the midst of this assembly? The assembly asks God to forgive the mould and sourness, the social injustice and to transform the imperfect gifts and return them to the assembly as the risen Just One. Does the assembly partake of these consecrated elements if they are indifferent to the cries of the poor locked in the cage of unjust social, economic and political structures?

f. The Collection/Offering

Collection is taken up at eucharistic celebration. The collected funds are frequently brought up to the table with the gifts of bread and wine in some places. Christians have always made contributions of goods and cash for the needs of the church and the poor. The collection of filthy lucre in worship is a powerful reminder that the christian life is not angelic but very much in the midst of this world of human making.

The collection at worship is also a potent reminder that the assembly is entwined in the economic, social and political orders of its nation as being God's people, endeavour to provide for what it needs to live out its christian faith: Sunday liturgy, funerals, schools, relief agencies, hospitals, homes for the elderly, and so forth. One can easily get caught in the injustices that warp the economic, social and political spheres of one's society.

So the simple ritual of dropping money into the basket or collection box at Sunday worship recalls one's responsibility to seek social justice in exercising the stewardship over this world's goods which God entrusts to all.[148] Indeed, the right to just wages and the sin of defrauding workers come to mind during collection. As the gifts are presented one can wonder about one's economic system which produces these gifts, a system which seems incapable of full employment and overcoming vast pockets of hungry and poor people in the midst of the most affluent nations in the world.

g. The Eucharistic Prayer

The Eucharistic prayer of the Church centres on asking God for peace and unity which are the prerequisites for social justice.[149] To pray for the unity of the church, therefore, is to pray for all of the factors which make up unity and all the virtues required to make them possible, including social justice. The

89

church within herself must lead in issues of social justice. Without social justice in the church, the equality of persons will not be acknowledged in fact; the diversity of gifts, ministries and works will not be utilised; and harmonious interaction will be replaced by favouritism, conflict and smothering of some members' gifts. Without ecclesial social justice, the divine intent for the body of Christ and fulfilment of the Eucharist will be frustrated. Furthermore, the church's purpose in the world, will be crippled.

Unless there is social justice in the church essential for its unity, the church cannot be an effective model or credible prophet to the world of the unity and implicitly, the social justice to which humanity is called. This does not just mean attitudes and deeds of individuals, but of the very way the church, the local parish, the diocese or presbytery or district, a church school or hospital, is organised and carries on its activities. Does the church in its structures as well as the habitual attitudes and actions of its members follow the social *status quo* of society, or does it challenge society with an example of social justice and unity.[150]

The Eucharistic prayers vision of the unity of all women and men raises questions about the international economic order, where certain developed nations hold other nations in economic dependence, so that the citizens of the former can enjoy luxuries to which they have become accustomed to, while citizens of the latter are deprived of their labours' fruits, which are siphoned off by the economic colonialists.

h. The Lord's Prayer

The Lord's Prayer, Our Father is replete with implications for social justice. The prayer draws the assembly out of themselves. The prayer reminds the assembly that they are a part of human family, to whom God has given creation, so that every human person has a right to life and the riches of nature and human invention. It further reminds us that all women and men are God's children for all of whom God created the earth, including future generations whom one can unjustly deprive of their heritage by polluting land, sea and air and recklessly consuming and wasting natural resources.

i. Prayer for Peace

Prayer for peace seeks to make peace an essential purpose of the eucharistic celebration. The peace in question means not only inner quiet of the soul, not only harmony between individuals, but also a social order in which each person enjoys a fair share of God's gifts to humanity in creation. The sign of peace given to those around become merely superficial if it is not accompanied by a willingness and appropriate action to provide justice for all in the parish, neighbourhood, cities, nation and world. The Hebrew word, *Shalom*, implies a fullness of blessing and happy relationships, all of which entails a just social order as a requisite element.[151]

At this juncture in the eucharistic celebration, the prayer for peace and sign of peace are occasions to recall the scourge of injustice inflicted on innocent children, women, and elderly by war and the robbery committed against the poor by the vast sums of money, labour and natural resources poured into making weapons of war.

x. Consumerism in Relation to Liturgy and Social Justice

Consumerism contributes to a very large extent as a social factor which prevents the assembly from hearing the eucharistic mandate of *Ite Missa est* in relation to social Justice. Consumerism generally refers to a complex of three factors.

i.   an economic system which places an extremely high value on the incessant production and consumption of material goods and services at an ever higher level of physical convenience and comfort.

ii. An accompanying mentality which assumes that such a system is the best or only one possible.

iii. A related tendency or even drive to find much, sometimes most, though rarely all, human fulfilment in providing and consuming these material goods and services.

Consumerism if not well checkmated with deep liturgical spirituality has the great potentiality to confound liturgy's message of social justice. Granted that liturgy and consumerism are un-associated in people's ordinary consciousness, their lives are lived and their liturgies are celebrated in the context of a consumer society. The suspicion arises therefore, that perhaps consumerism influences the liturgy in unconscious ways and thus prevents the liturgy from being authentically christian worship, and ultimately prohibits the hearing of its message of social justice.

xi. Globalisation in Relation to Liturgy and Social Justice

Ite Missa est proffers some soothing answers regarding the question of Eucharist and Globalisation. In dealing with Eucharist and Globalisation ones attention is drawn to a new concept that hitherto seems to be very much neglected. This is rather a new approach to the Eucharist because it links the members not only with one another as believers but also to non believers in a most intimate manner. Eucharistic globalisation has very many positive implications for peace, social justice and unity in the world today.

One simply needs to recall that the Eucharist is the essence of christian praxis, the fulfilment of baptism, a thankful yes to Jesus' life, death and resurrection which incorporates the members as a spirited community to do as Jesus did, to strive and build the kingdom of God. One of the mistakes often in the approach to Eucharist is to allow too individualistic and therapeutic emphasis on real presence to obscure the deeper meaning of Christ's presence and action in the members as a community of believers. It was St. Augustine who rightly said, we eat the body of Christ to become the body of Christ. A lot of implications flow from this in this new Millennium? Today one requires a much broadened view and extended approach to what Christ is to the members and to the larger society.

First of all, the received meanings of Eucharist in the face of globalisation, need to be teased out: global covenant community, thanksgiving, sacrifice, reconciliation, table ministry and the banquet of human destiny. If a little piece of the globe: bread and wine, fruit of the vine and work of human hands, can be Christ's presence, then so can the rest of the universe. It was Michael Himes who says that the Eucharist is the tip of the iceberg. It is the first step in the transubstantiation of all creation which is the destiny of the universe.[152]

St. Paul in 1 Cor. 11:17-34 underscored this global application very succinctly. Here Paul was seeking to get to the root of the insensitive behaviour of the Corinthians. Their understanding was very much tied up with an individuated Christ, in that there was little or no grasp of being members of one another in a whole which is his sacred presence. They failed to understand the Eucharist as the presence that unites members in the body and creates a single entity. Their belief was in a disembodied Jesus.

Paul aims for the deeper meaning of the real presence as the Body of Christ identified with the community. His concern gets behind interpersonal behaviour as well as racial, national, economic, ideological and social divisions. He invites them to a discernment process of self examination around the Eucharist. He reminds the Corinthian community that Jesus said he would be there in the poor, the prisoner and the foreigner and then raises the Trinitarian dimension that Christ wishes that they all may be one in us. Paul's views touched political, economic, and environmental issues.

Pope John Paul II, strongly maintained that without defence of the poor and marginalised, both individuals and nations, globalisation could end up being merely a new and perhaps more deadly form of colonialism.[153] Paul's concerns are equally local and global: Examine yourself, and only then eat of the bread and drink of the cup. For all who eat and drink without discerning the body, eat and drink judgement against themselves. A renewed sense of Paul's embodied Eucharist is needed to infuse a global Catholicism capable of being incorporated in each culture, yet open to the potential goods of a global culture.

Globalisation means a united world, a relational wholeness, one to all, one for all, what happens to one happens to all or affects all. The problem of one is the problem of all. It is solidarity. In this context, Eucharist makes real the presence of Christ both in the elements and in the body of believers. Eucharist is the interior retreat, a spiritual thing. In the Eucharist, the members put on Christ and relive his story and in doing that, discover themselves more closely. This is what the assembly is called to do at every Eucharist. Such an approach implemented within the context of the eucharistic presence as relational wholeness could ignite communities to take up difficult socio-economic questions.[154]

xii.   Conclusion

The eucharistic liturgy transcends the immediate environment in its effect to become the inspirational force for christian activists in the social order. The expectations from the eucharistic celebration demand that the participants never remain the same as they were before and after the encounter with the Lord. The Eucharist which still remains a simple but sumptuous meal that nourishes the members for soul and body wellbeing has equally a great thrust to nourish and influence a great deal the social values of the larger society.

The same Jesus who sent out the disciples out to go and proclaim the good news after having groomed and nourished them with his word, remains the same minister of the Eucharist who dismisses the eucharistic assembly through the priest to the same mission of caring for souls, mind and body. The small scale missionaries of Christ's time have today multiplied in thousands and millions bearing the same message of making him known, present and loveable to the larger society and to transform the world values into christian values.

The world today is in dire need of peace, unity and justice. These have constantly eluded the world today. These values could be re-cultivated by recourse to the sacrament of unity, peace and justice as contained in the Eucharist.

In the eucharistic mandate, the church is expected to complete the work of Christ on earth by continuing to carry on the mission which he began while he was on earth. This includes the mission of announcing the good news to the poor, freedom to captives and joy to mourners. Jesus sends the Holy Spirit to believers to make them his ecclesial body in space and time and to inspire them to carry out this mission, his mission. Jesus, through his members, brings the fullness of grace to men and women down through the ages and ultimately through the consummation of creation on the last Day. A significant factor in completing Jesus' work is struggling for social justice, even as it implies love, humility and other virtuous attitudes and activities.

Ite Missa est at the end of every eucharistic celebration is not only a statement about what may have occurred personally in the course of the celebration just completed, it is also the beginning of a mission, or the renewal of a mission, to seek that social justice which corresponds to God's reign on earth as in heaven.

As the participants take their exit, they go to embrace and tackle social justice issues in the larger society.

Ite Missa est is a joyful parting farewell. It sends the church forth to work for a condition of human life and society which can be achieved only if the citizens vote conscientiously for political leaders who are dedicated to fashioning just economic, social and political structures in the society and in the international community. Our discussion can be very aptly summed up in a popular local hymn as follows:

Go, you Christians, the Mass is ended!

Go into the world, to sanctify the world!

You are the light of the world, the children of God!

Show all people, the truth of God!

CHAPTER FOUR:

Eucharistic Liturgy:
The Undying Hope of the Church

i.   Introduction

As a celebration *par excellence,* eucharistic liturgy means the celebration of the Eucharist as the public worship of the mystical body of Christ[155] with the paschal mystery of Christ [156] as its content where every member performs his or role or ministries optimally equipped with proper liturgical books and tools. It is that unique celebration which every other celebrations in the church look up to or regard as their summit and source.[157] Such a celebration requires as a matter of necessity, the presidency of the clergy and the active participation of the laity. Other liturgical celebrations of the Church would ordinarily include the other sacraments and other celebrations acclaimed liturgical by the Church.[158]

St. Paul in his Exhortation on spiritual worship, offers the Church a meaningful spiritual approach to the celebration of these liturgical celebrations when he rightly says: I urge you, then, brothers, remembering the mercies of God, to offer your bodies as a living sacrifice, dedicated and acceptable to God; that is the kind of worship for you as sensible people.[159]

Christ perfectly justified this text through his paschal mystery as an eloquent example for his mystical body to follow suit. For that indeed, is what the Church is called to be and to do in (*anamnesis-mimesis-metasxesis -martyria* (Gk)) the form of re-enactment-imitation-participation through witnessing in practical life to the Lord and Master. What is very much in question here is having the true spirit of worship.

All who received baptism belong to the Church in which all are first born sons and daughters without discrimination. All are members in the Church as true sons and daughters. All are incorporated in the Church as co-heirs with Christ the Lord. As participants through baptism, all receive the signs and gifts of that great vocation which enables one and obliges one even in the midst of human weakness to seek perfection (cf. 2 Cor. 12:9). As full members of the Church through baptism, our incorporation into Christ demands the celebration of the entire mysteries of Christ. It presupposes the celebration of who and what Christ is in whole not in part.

Catholics incidentally belong to the Church in which not only the whole truth subsists[160] but the entire mysteries of Christ are celebrated. They belong to the Church which is often hated or despised by all those who are alien to the truth of the Eucharist. Nevertheless, it is the Church which is modelled according to the *Ecclesia* in Africa as a family of God. A church-family which has father, mother and children with mutual respect and love for each other; a church-family where the role of the father is very well underscored; a church-family where the mother's role is also very well articulated; a church-family where the children are adequately highlighted and given a place of belonging, incorporation, participation and membership through the three sacraments of initiation: Baptism, Confirmation and the holy Eucharist.

The Incarnation incidentally stresses these roles very succinctly. The infant Jesus was not deprived of a mother and a foster father. The belief in the nomenclatures, the holy Mother Church and the Holy Father which the church uses when referring to the motherhood and fatherhood of the church comes into focus. These nomenclatures provide a most suitable homely setting for greater appreciation and celebration of the Eucharistic Liturgy. The separated brethren neither believe in the Holy Mother Church, in the Holy Mother of God nor in the Holy Father. Catholics however, who believe in these ought to behave as those who have both a spiritual Father and a spiritual Mother especially towards themselves and then to the separated brethren. In the spirit of ecumenism, true love, fervent prayer, mutual understanding and authentic witnessing could be possible channels of reconciliation and unity.

One can hardly ignore the extra-ordinary experience obtainable in the places of worship belonging to the separated brethren. Such an experience is very much like what happened on the resurrection morning at the tomb of Christ Jesus. The emphasis here is on Christ to emphasis his divinity. It belongs to the tradition of the classical Latin rite to qualify Jesus in the liturgy.[161] One could count so many Jesuses in the bible according to biblical scholars and sources. Some of these Jesuses even opposed the spread of the gospel of Christ. [162]

On that Sunday morning, the first day of the week, the day of the Resurrection, the women came to the tomb to anoint the body, the angel told them, *he is not here*. This is exactly the way one feels, on entering into the churches of these separated brethren. The absence of the light and the tabernacle with the veil quickly announce, *he is not here*! [163] He is risen, alive and present. Where then is he? Where they left him namely, in the Church. Whenever one loses Christ, one would always find him where one left him. Mary and Joseph lost Jesus in the temple after the feast in Jerusalem. [164] When they were looking for him, they found him in the temple, the very place they lost him. So he is there in the Church: on the Altar, under the appearance of Bread and Wine: Body and Blood, the Eucharist.

A great deal of thrill goes with the simple definition of the Church as the People of God for it connects every believer very easily with Israel; the *Qahal Yahweh*. One feels very much excited with the kind of assembly Christ meant when he says that where two or three are gathered in his name, he is there in their midst. [165]

The technical definition of the Church certainly goes beyond this generalised concept. The Church is surely more than an assemblage of people in the name of Christ. A church where people merely gather to pray, to sing, preach powerfully behind extra mega microphones, make cash offerings, play melodious rhythms, exchange sweet pleasantries, share brotherhood, and exercise hospitality etc, can very well be described as a congregational church. Catholics are more than mere congregational church. They are Eucharistic Church for it is indeed the Eucharist that makes the Church. Without the Eucharist there is no Church, and no priesthood, just as without the Church there is no Eucharist and priesthood, and without the priesthood there is no Eucharist, for he the priest alone can vicariously (for Christ) confect the Eucharist which makes the Church.

When Christ Jesus was leaving for heaven, he left only one Peter, with only one bunch of keys. There could be many roads leading to the Kingdom but there is only one way, and there is only one man with the key. Against this backdrop therefore, it becomes only reasonable to insist on following the man with the key. And Christ even told them, I am with you even until the end of time. That was not just a promise, but rather a statement of fact. He is there already: the *Immanuel,* so the Incarnation is continuing using the Church to reach out and to save the world. Calvary is also continuing seen in those who suffer directly and or indirectly for Christ and with him for the salvation of the world: the innocent for instance who suffer, the just who are victimised, etc.

Many Catholics today seem to be disturbed and sometimes discouraged by the apparent mass exodus of the members who go out to swell the numerical strength of the Pentecostal and Protestant churches. No doubt that some Catholics could be responsible for the exodus in some way, for this is only human and only portrays the human face of the church.

The Good news today is that as much as you have the exodus from the Catholic church there is equal or even more influx into the Catholic Church today. One observes this particularly at the confessional and in the rapid multiplication of parishes. A lot who have left have discovered that the truth subsists in the Catholic Church and those of them who are humble enough return en masse and never to leave. Their return remains permanent.

The celebrations of the Church have never been a buffet. It has never been a matter of pick and choose. It is a matter of either you take it *in toto* or you leave it entirely. It is a matter of firm decision. It is very much like what happened in John 6: 66-7, *will you also go away?* To the rich young man who came to Jesus for spiritual direction, Jesus said, *sell all you have, give the money to the poor and come follow me* (Mk. 10:22ff). As the young man was leaving, Christ never called him back to compromise what he said or to mitigate the sternness of his teaching on discipleship.

The true cost of discipleship demands self renunciation and a total surrender to the lordship of Jesus. It is even more than making sacrifices or giving up particular interest or possession. It is a demand for a radical re-orientation of life with self no longer at the centre. The Will of God, as known through Christ must take the place of our own wills. Hence Jesus said, my meat is to do the will of him who sent me and to accomplish his work.[166] Jesus demands that we habitually think of others, only occasionally remembering ourselves. Self-denial may even demand the supreme sacrifice of one's life.

Indeed, there has been no time in history when the total submission to Christ, his teachings and the celebration of his entire mysteries have been tried and found impossible, but they have never been found to be easy. It is a religion that costs much. It did cost blood. It did cost someone his life. Because a religion that costs nothing produces practically nothing.

There are so many things other churches borrow from the Church: searching the scriptures, singing hymns, use of terminology like parish, rectory, tithe etc. Unfortunately the irony of it all is that many of the Catholics today with their worthy self-esteemed liturgy seems to be having a negative borrowing tendency and a kind of inferiority complex. Instead of being the object of admiration, the Church seems to be an admirer within the theatre of multiple competitors. It is very much like in Igbo culture of (*Ijelle putara n'ogbo kwulu kilibe ulaga*) a very big masquerade like *Ijelle* that takes so much time, cost and labour to prepare that came to the market square to display but turns to admire the tiny children's masquerade like *ulaga*.

The Charismatic renewal is not in question here. The Church in Nigeria for instance must be deeply indebted to the Charismatic Renewal for giving her a new and prosperous way of conducting effective and maximum-result-oriented offertory collection today. The secret bag collection method has now giving way to choruses that move people from the seats to donate generously as they move to the altar. The Church's form of worship is far more than that. The one area where other churches fail to imitate the Catholic Church is her liturgy particularly the eucharistic liturgy.

Certainly the reason for this is more than mere externals. The reason is not far fetched. It is because Christ is involved. Sacrifice is involved. Priesthood is involved. Victimhood is involved. Mediation is involved. Something is broken. Something precious is poured out.

Prior to this time, a priest is someone who offers something on behalf of others. The pagan priesthood, the Jewish priesthood all offered something outside of themselves, goats, yams, chickens, libations, sometimes children. In the case of Christ, he was more than a priest, he was both priest and victim. He offered himself as the victim of sacrifice. He has always combined these two realities without dichotomy: priesthood and victimhood: holiness and identification with the suffering humanity. A man like us in all things but sin. That was why his unique sacrifice was once and for all, acceptable and irrepeatable. What priests do today is not a repetition but a re-enactment, *anamnesis,* a sacrifice which God cannot but receive for it will be a contradiction for God to reject himself in Christ.

So the proud legacy of the Church among other churches and religions is because she celebrates the Eucharist as a memorial of the paschal mystery of Christ in a most excellent way as well as other sacraments of Christ. This is where the burden of this discussion lies.

There is the need to find out what implications flow from this as they affect the Church in her members as individuals in their respective vocations within the same Church. What is the Eucharist for each and everyone? Does it really mean bread broken for others, and wine poured out for others? Is it a continuing event or is it just done and finished with? Do the members really know what they are celebrating and worshipping as Christ demanded in Jn. 4:23ff: you worship what you do not know, we worship what we do know. Has this broken body any implications for the Church in her members? For instance, as priests ordained specifically for the continuous celebration of the Eucharist until the Lord returns, is the eucharistic celebration really a re-enactment of this mystery? How does one appreciate the entire liturgy of the Church? And for the laity, does it really mean making a genuine spiritual offering with full, active and conscious participation in it?

ii.   Interiorisation of the Liturgical Celebrations

As Christ fittingly asked in the above Johannine text, how fully convinced is the Church in her members: clergy and laity in the liturgical celebrations entrusted to them? What is the level of commitment to the mysteries she celebrates especially the Eucharist? What efforts are being made to appropriate the fruits of the celebrations as to become part and parcel of both the celebrants and the participants.

May be the Church in her members needs to be clearly reminded that the liturgical celebrations are special salvific responsibilities given to her by Christ.

These celebrations are mysteries of Christ entrusted to the priests to celebrate with specific instructions on how to celebrate them (like the manual of a motor car) with the ultimate aim of achieving the total transformation, sanctification, edification of the people of God, and for the glorification of God.

The mysteries belong exclusively to Christ himself and he determines through the Church how best to celebrate them for his mystical body. The mysteries are more than an individual or individuals put together. They are not a question of mine nor yours to do as we like. Faithful observance of the rules is very much in question at this point. Intelligent observance of liturgical laws forms an integral part of the vow of obedience for the priests and religious.

Against this background, the observance of the norms published by the authority of the Church requires conformity of thought and of word, of external actions and of application of the heart. A merely external observation of norms would obviously be contrary to the true nature of the Sacred Liturgy, in which Christ himself wishes to gather his Church, so that together with himself she will be one body and one spirit. For this reason, external actions must be illumined by faith and charity, which unite us with Christ and with one another and engender love for the poor and the abandoned. The liturgical words and rites, moreover, are a faithful expression, matured over the centuries, of the understanding of Christ, and they teach us to think as he himself does; by conforming our minds to these words, as we raise our hearts to the Lord.[167]

iii.   Reformed Liturgy of the Second Vatican Council

The liturgy has been the starting point of constant reformation and renewal of the life of the Church. No wonder then, the Fathers of the Second Vatican Council wisely began the reforms of the life of the Church with the Church's liturgy leading to the emergence of the first document called the *Sacrosanctum Concilium* - Document on the Sacred Liturgy in March 19, 1965.

The liturgy has always been considered to be the life-wire and the nerve-centre of the Church. Indeed, the vitality of any local Church can always be assessed by the pulse of her worshipping forms. Liturgy however, does not exhaust the entire activity of the Church.[168] It remains however, *the culmen et fons*, the apex and source of the christian life and spirituality.[169] By the liturgical reforms, the Council Fathers aimed at achieving the maximum active, conscious, plenary and socio-Communitarian participation of the faithful in the Liturgy.[170] At the same time, the Church's liturgy must not be complicated or become cumbersome. It must be distinguished by noble simplicity, brevity, sobriety and practicality.[171]

With regard to liturgical inculturation, the Church does not stifle initiatives, rather it boosts individual's or people's cultural values and genius of the people and encourages same to be admitted into the liturgy. However, such innovations or initiatives have to be subjected to the proper ecclesiastical authority for approval and implementation.[172] Furthermore, the Church's liturgy is not in favour of having only one way of doing the same thing by everyone. There has to be unity in essence but diversity in expression: oneness in plurality. Therefore, while maintaining the substantial unity of the faith, it has to be expressed in different forms according to people's cultural way.[173]

The reformed liturgy of the Second Vatican Council is very much open to creativity, innovations, creation of alternatives and encourages even total replacement with entirely new rites over and above the ones contained in the typical editions. Against this backdrop, local Churches have been given almost an unlimited liberty or latitude in the area of liturgical inculturation of marriage rites to create or evolve either alternative rites or even an entirely new rites to replace those contained in the typical editions.[174]

iv. Council's Reforms Must Be Part of Believer's Lives

In August 12, 2003, the Holy Father, Pope John Paul II, sent a letter to the Italian National Liturgy Week Members Commemorating the fortieth Anniversary of the publication of the Constitution on the Sacred Liturgy, *Sacrosanctum Concilium*. In that letter, the Holy Father recalled his famous statement at the twenty fifth anniversary of the same document *SC.*, thus, the liturgy's reform was in harmony with the general hope of the whole Church. In fact, the liturgical spirit has become widespread together with the desire for an active participation in the most holy mysteries and in the public and prayer life of the Church.[175]

The liturgical reform gave new vitality to Christian life. The liturgy has helped people to move in the right direction especially by following faithfully the guiding principles of the Constitution and has remained the primary and indispensable source of true christian spirit.[176] Furthermore, the liturgical reform has led to a new and intensified education in order to discover all the richness contained in the liturgy. The reform should be translated into the lives of the believers as well as establish communion between the people and the mystery they celebrate.[177]

One of the new approaches to the liturgy must be pastoral for an on going commitment. The church ought to put the liturgy first as the *summit* and *source* of the Church's action. Specific areas to be considered in liturgy today include, the relationship between spiritual worship and life, catechesis and celebration of the paschal mystery, presiding at the liturgy and the role of the congregation, seminary formation and continuing formation of the priests in the liturgy.[178] At the end, the Holy Father, assured the members of his remembrance in prayer for the success of their work, and hopes that the deviations and the liberties taken, that were often caused by an inability to grasp the proper spirit of the liturgical reform may be corrected.[179] So the Holy Father acknowledges the aberrations and abuses taking place in the liturgy today on a global scale.

v.   Centrality of the Eucharistic in Christian Worship

a. A Brief Historical Overview

Historically, the Church has through the centuries safeguarded the centrality of the Eucharist in her liturgical life.[180] In celebrating the Eucharist, the Church has always demonstrated her openness to the cultural values and genius of the cultures of peoples. Christ was the first inculturator. He established the sacrament of the Eucharist of his body and blood in the process of an on-going Jewish pass over meal as seen at the beginning. As a protagonist of authentic inculturation, he applied the principle which he formulated himself, namely, he came not to abolish the law and the prophets rather to fulfil them (Matt.

5:17); he came not to destroy but to build up, he came to give life in abundance (cf. Jn. 10:10), starting with the life giving bread and blood of himself.

b. Era of the Primitive Church

In the early Church, the apostles took after their master. They remained faithful to the Lord's teaching and command. The apostles and others would pray ordinarily like every other Jew in the synagogues but they would retire later into private homes for the celebration of the Eucharist (cf. Acts. 2:46). In Acts 1:13, one hears about the upper room in which the Eucharist was celebrated.

In the age of persecution, on account of the hostilities of the persecutors, the apostolic practice of celebrating the breaking of bread, *fractio panis* in private homes, catacombs was institutionalised. The well to do members in the early Church offered their houses for the use of the *Ekklesia*, the worshipping community. For instance, the Roman *tablinium*, where the *pater familias* presided, the *atrium* where the members of the family assembled, the *triclinium* or dinning room and the *implivium* which was a large tank of water were a perfect set up for the eucharistic celebration.[181] For the early Church the celebration of the Eucharist was central in their life.

c. The Greeco - Roman Era

The era featured prominently such celebrations as Easter, Sunday, Christian Initiation and Praises. At the heart and centre of these celebrations was the eucharistic celebration which was structured and patterned after the Eighteen Blessings in the Jewish prayer *(Shemone Esre Berakot)*. In the Christian context, the Jewish Prayer was imbued and enriched with Christian signification namely, the eucharistic contents. Furthermore, the whole effort of the Church to change her language from *koine* Greek to Latin was all with the intention of comprehending better the eucharistic celebration thus leading to better and more meaningful celebration of the Eucharist.

d. The Era of Emperor Constantine

With the conversion of Emperor Constantine in AD 313 and the subsequent edict of Milan in AD 314, there came an end to the hostile and fierce persecutions of the Christians and thus marking the dawn of an era of freedom and independence for the Church. In order to boost liturgical celebrations whose chief act was the Eucharist, the Emperor after his conversion and the subsequent influx of new converts to the Church (for the religion of the Emperor became largely the religion of the empire as a co-operate personality), he bequeathed some of his administrative buildings to the Church to offer adequate accommodation for all. These civil administrative edifices were then converted into basilicas. His conversion and generosity led to a tremendous increase in the numerical strength of the faithful in the celebration of the Eucharist.[182]

Sunday was understood as the weekly (*anamnesis*) remembrance of the Lord's resurrection, the day of the Lord, the day of the assembly and the day of celebration of the Eucharist. At this period, Sunday became popularised and recognised as a work free day by the state. Easter being a yearly re-enactment of the supreme victory of Christ over death in his resurrection, became a prolonged fifty days celebration culminating at the Pentecost. Lent assumed a liturgical role of being a preparatory period for the Easter celebration with penitence, catechumenate exercise and celebration of the Eucharist as its most essential content. Furthermore, Christmas became a reaction and divinisation of *dies natalis solis invicti*-the day of the unconquerable sun, to become the birthday of Christ. At the heart of this celebration also was the Eucharist.

e. The Pure Liturgical Era of the Seventh Century

Also referred to as the classical liturgical era in liturgical history, saw the eucharistic celebration as dominating the entire scene of all liturgical celebrations. The eucharistic celebration was distinguished by noble simplicity, brevity, sobriety and practicality.[183] The splendour of the eucharistic celebration was occasioned by a number of reasons ranging from the availability of pure and proper liturgical books and each liturgical functionary performed their roles dutifully well. The Church even in her subsequent liturgical renewals has always looked upon this epoch as the standard in liturgical celebrations with special reference to the Eucharist.

f. The Franco - Germanic Era of the Eighth Century

When Roman liturgy met some crisis it needed to be salvaged. The crisis came from clashes of interest between the Popes and the Emperors and the latter no longer promoted liturgy as before. Other problems arose from the incomprehensibility of the language of the liturgy, upsurge of private devotions during eucharistic celebrations, personal approach to the eucharistic liturgy on the part of the clergy, the position of the celebrant at such celebrations in which he stood between the altar and the people. Consequently the people became distant from the liturgical actions that took place and the degree of participation in the liturgy was reduced drastically.

Two prominent figures featured in this era, King Pepin and his son Charles the Great. The former sought for the unification of the kingdom through the Roman liturgical book. Unable to accomplish this before his death, his son took it over and what he received from Rome was the Hadrian Gregorian Sacramentary *(Sacramentarium Gregorianum Hadrianum)* which was very limited in scope and contents.

Secondly it was found to be inadequate to suit and satisfy the sentiments of the Franco-Germanic people. It was so limited in scope and failed to cover the major aspects of the people's way of life. When the *Sacramentarium Hadrianum* migrated into the Franco Germanic world, it came in contact with already existing liturgical books namely, the Gallican and Gelasian liturgy thus giving rise to a mixture of Roman-Hadrianum; Roman-Gelasianum and Gallican. The mixed liturgy was intended to enhance the comprehension of the liturgical celebration. What eventually became the fate of that gift from Rome was first to fill up the lacunae by experts like Alcuin the Abbot of Tours who was also the King's adviser.

With his expertise assistance in liturgical matters he enriched the deficient book with the creditable values and the genius of the Franco-Germanic people. When the book later went back to Rome at around AD 1000, it was found to be completely Franco-germanised.[184] The experience of the Franco Germanic people serves as a veritable precedence worthy of emulation by subsequent agents of liturgical inculturation.

g. The Middle Ages 10th – 16th Centuries

On account of liturgical decadence in Rome, caused by the reasons already given in the preceding section, the Roman Franco Germanic liturgy had to return to Rome to form the basis of the Roman liturgy of the middle ages. The liturgical life of the time was essentially based on the theology of transubstantiation. People attended Mass only to experience the changing of bread and wine into the body and blood of Christ as they are being elevated.

The desire to see the host constituted the most important aspect of participation at the eucharistic celebration. Propitiatory sacrifice was another important aspect the eucharistic celebration that formed the liturgical spirituality of the era.

Hence as many Masses as possible were being offered for various intentions. Private masses were very much on the increase. Many faceted masses were rampant on account of many mass stipends. Ordination to the priesthood was on the high increase in order to cope with the demands of saying many masses. Even many monks became ordained as priests to assist in the increasing demands for man power in the celebration of many masses. Masses could even be said in absentia, in which the donor or the one who booked for the mass needed not to be present as the mass was being celebrated.

Kultur Latin language which was considered to be the language of the elite as opposed to common Latin as the language of the eucharistic celebration became increasingly difficult to comprehend thus leading to diminishing participation in the celebrations, promotion of private devotions during eucharistic celebration and ultimately ushered in the age of clericalism.

Nevertheless, the Eucharist never lost its pride of place in the liturgical life of the Church. The consequent reformation that took place as a result of this anomaly attacked the Church by denying the sacrificial anamnetical nature of the Eucharist as well as the real presence of Christ in the host during and after consecration of the hosts.

h. The Tridentine Era

The counter reformation came up and took steps to correct the errors of the reformers through the able agency of the Council of Trent. The Council started by clarifying the position of the Church on the issues at hand. It defined the sacrificial value of the Eucharist and clarified the legitimacy of the rites which celebrate it. It attempted to reverse the interest of the people from a dissatisfied, discordant and chaotic liturgy to the spirit of the liturgy through carefully worded definitions, decrees and canons on the Eucharist.

The Council made further attempts to streamline liturgical worship into a refined and purified form of worship. Judged in its context, the Council had so many positive values to its credits especially through the sharp opposition against Protestantism, underscoring the sacrificial character of the eucharistic celebration, the importance of the real presence, the codification of the liturgical books and attempting to create a liturgy that was pastoral and within the reach of the people.

Conversely, the Council was found to be codifying an already out-dated liturgy that did not correspond to the spiritual cultural context of the people. Consequently, the Council was protecting a form of liturgy that distanced itself from the people since the degree of liturgical participation was still very low.

i. Post Tridentine Liturgical Periods - Era of Baroque

The apparent fixity and rigors of Trent brought about the Baroquean epoch,[185] which came to mitigate the rigidity of Trent. Within the period, the Church had a kind of quiet breathing space and security. Most of the debatable points of disagreements became clarified; the life and activity of the clergy became regulated, liturgical books were published and the rubrics were strictly adhered to and new religious orders and prominent Bishops like Charles Boromeo emerged. Baroque of course had no liturgy peculiar to it.

Nevertheless, with Baroque music, arts, festivities, processions and senti-ments spread their gorgeous mantle over liturgical celebrations especially the Eucharist. The era was thus judged by the subsequent era as very sentimental, external, and unintelligently traditionalistic. Thus it needed to be succeeded by another form of mentality known as illuminism or Enlightenment of the eighteenth century.

j. Era of Illuminism

Illuminism was regarded as a theologico-political movement planned against the festivities and sentimentalism of the Baroquean era. It opted for the freedom from all excesses and emotions in the liturgical celebrations, as well as super-fluous forms and insisted on the return of the liturgy to a noble simplicity of the primitive Church. It advocated that arts and music should return to the noble simplicity of the classical era. It opted for a consolidation and activation of the congregation based on the enlightenment of the faithful.

There should be one Mass in the parish Church for all the parishioners together with homily and communion for all. Musical instruments were to be abolished in the liturgical celebrations except perhaps on feast days to allow for intellectual exercises in the celebration, a kind of contemplative or meditation-filled celebrations. Priests celebrants must face the people. There should be no rosary recitations or private devotions during eucharistic celebrations. Restrains should be applied in the exposition of the Blessed Sacrament.

Reformation was necessary with regard to offertory procession, kiss of peace and concelebration. Illuminism failed at the end to open the door to the heart of the liturgy as the liturgy was still estranged from the people. It was too humanistic, individualistic, subjective and intellectualistic.The eucharistic celebration became too cerebral rather than being pastoral and spiritual.

k. Era of Restoration

From eighteenth century onwards, up until the period of Restoration in the nineteenth century not much of liturgical growth and development were recorded. The term Restoration was rather found to be a misnomer in the sense that this period marked another era of liturgical decadence in the annals of worship. Liturgy was almost dormant.

The inability of the liturgy to address the problematic issues of the period was very remarkable. Liturgical celebration especially the Eucharist became a merely fixed monument, whose only concern was the re-affirmation of the resolutions of Council of Trent. It became an era of worn-out liturgy as well as an era without grace and without any significant creativity.

A ray of hope appeared with the emergence of the movement called the liturgical movements which was championed by eminent liturgical scholars like P. Gueranger, L. Beaudium, and Odo Casel etc.The movement was understood as a sign of God's providence, a breath of the Spirit into the Church and a start of a new life. It was this movement indeed that paved the way for the reforms of the Second Vatican Council.

Throughout the entire history of the church as reviewed the Eucharist never lost its centrality. At one time the centrality was outstanding and at other times it was besieged with abuses which never denied it of its uses. The abuses and the consequent reactions against the defaulters even made the Church to reassure herself of her doctrinal positions, reaffirm her faith in the Eucharist and propose ways of enhancing the dignity and centrality of the Eucharist.

vi.   Centrality of the Eucharist in the Other Sacraments

When one speaks of the centrality of the Eucharist in relation to the other sacraments, one wishes to highlight the Eucharist as the summit and fountain- *culmen et fons*[186] of other sacraments as well as all the other celebrations of the Church. The term summit (*culmen*) refers to that apex that every sacrament attains which is always in the eucharistic celebration.

The celebration of each of the sacraments reaches its climatic point, its summit, its apex in the celebration of the Eucharist. All the sacraments are Eucharist oriented. All tilt towards the Eucharist to arrive at the supreme goal. In effect, the eucharistic celebration brings to culmination the celebration of any such sacrament.

The term fountain, *fons* refers to the aftermath of the celebration. It deals with what takes place after reaching the apex of the celebration in the Eucharist. It means precisely that the Eucharist which marks the apex of the celebration remains at the same time the source, the well spring of power for sustenance in the life of grace received. The Eucharist provides the source of nourishment, graces and virtues necessary for perseverance in facing courageously the challenges related to the sacrament just celebrated.

Against this background therefore, the Eucharist has a continuous function that produces on-going effects. Hence one of the reasons for the appellation that among all the sacraments, the Eucharist is the sacrament *par excellence*. It remains the centre of the Church's life.[187] The close nexus between the Eucharist and other sacraments could well be illustrated thus:

a. Sacraments of Christian Initiation

These ordinarily include Baptism, Confirmation and the Eucharist. They form a single act in three stages in the process of making a full Christian. They lay the foundations of every Christian life. The sharing in the divine nature given to human beings through the grace of Christ bears a certain likeness to the origin, development and nourishing of natural life. The faithful are born anew by baptism, strengthened by the sacrament of Confirmation, and receive in the Eucharist the food of eternal life.

By means of these sacraments of Christian initiation, they thus receive in increasing measure the treasures of the divine life and advance towards the perfection of charity.[188] The Eucharist completes Christian initiation.

Those who have been raised to the dignity of the royal priesthood by Baptism, and configured more deeply to Christ by Confirmation, participate with the whole community in the Lord's own sacrifice by means of the Eucharist.[189] The Eucharist which forms the apex of Christian initiation remains at the same time the source through which the Christian life is constantly nourished.

b. Penance and Reconciliation

Sin is before all else an offence against God, a rupture of communion with God. At the same time it damages communion with the Church.[190] The sinner in actual fact wounds God's honour and love, his or her own human dignity as a person called to be a child of God, and the spiritual well being of the Church of which each Christian ought to be a living stone.[191]

A sinner therefore offends in three ways: against God, against oneself and against the Church. The three-tier severed relationship is thereby redressed through the process of true contrition, confession, satisfaction and absolution of sins. The climax of the reconciliation process comes with the reception of the Eucharist which thus seals the entire process (summit). The graces of perseverance, steadfastness that guarantees non-relapses are well provided by the same Eucharist as the source (fountain) of strength.

c. Anointing of the Sick

By the sacred anointing of the sick and the prayer of the priests the whole Church commends those who are ill to the suffering and glorified Lord, that he may raise them up and save them. And indeed she exhorts them to contribute to the good of the People of God by freely uniting themselves to the Passion and death of Christ.[192]

The sacrament is administered through prayers and anointing with the oil of the sick which could effect spiritual and physical healing. The culminating point of this celebration is the reception of the Eucharist *(culmen)*. At the same time, the same Eucharist acts as a means of constant strength, endurance and fortitude. And if one must die, it becomes a means of strength for the journey to ones homeland, serving as food for the wayfarer *(viaticum)*.

d. Holy Orders

Holy Orders is the sacrament through which the mission entrusted by Christ to his apostles continues to be exercised in the Church until the end of time: thus it is the sacrament of apostolic ministry.[193] The Church designates the three ministerial services as sacraments of holy orders with three degrees of the episcopacy, priesthood and diaconate. In these three degrees of ecclesiastical service, one is in each case ordained as a minister after the choice of the Church. They are called ministerial in order to ensure the unbroken proclamation and prolongation of the celebration of the paschal mystery of Christ to all ages.[194]

Their role is quite different from the baptismal priesthood. The redemptive sacrifice of Christ is unique, accomplished once and for all yet it is made present in the eucharistic sacrifice which is present through the ministerial priesthood without diminishing the uniqueness of Christ's priesthood. For only Christ is the true priest, the others being only his ministers.[195]

The celebration of each of these degrees in ecclesiastical services comes to a climax at the eucharistic celebration – *culmen*. Having won the *battle* to arrive at the ordination, one requires a *sustained war* to be able to survive as an ordained minister. The source of power and strength for the sustained war comes from the Eucharist as source, *fons*.

e. Matrimony

By Matrimony a man and a woman establish between themselves a lifetime partnership, which is by its nature ordered towards the good of the themselves, the procreation and education of their offspring. This covenant between baptised persons has been raised by Jesus to the dignity of a sacrament.[196] Furthermore, they signify and share in the mystery of that unity and fruitful love which exists between Christ and the Church (cf. Eph. 5:32).

The celebration of marriage involves exchange of consent and nuptial blessing. The fullness of the celebration of marriage comes with the Eucharist as the summit, *culmen*. The christian couple hereafter nourishes and develops their marriage by undivided affection which wells up from the fountain, *fons* of divine love which is the Eucharist and consequently keeps them faithful in body, soul and mind, in good times and in bad (cf. I Cor. 7:7).

What the Eucharist is for all the sacraments applies to all the other liturgical celebrations of the Church like the dedication of Churches and Altars, the sacramental celebrations of the Church like the Religious professions. The same applies to the paraliturgical and devotional activities of the Church. All these have the Eucharist as their summit and source *(culmen et fons)*.

vii.   Some Specific Areas in the Liturgy That Raise Concern

a. Faithful Observance of Liturgical Laws

Church's worship is meant to be well ordered. Liturgical law exists and is binding. But the purpose of this law is to encourage and promote the spiritual well-being, participation and unity of Christ's faithful. It also exists for the sanctification and protection of the clergy, who celebrate the rites of the Church at the very heart of their ministry to others. It is thus a law of service, not of servitude or to be followed sheepishly or mechanically.

It is not a law under the pain of facing a firing squad. It is rather of conscience. It is a law that flourishes only within the freedom of grace, because it facilitates the supreme ministry of grace, imparted in the sacraments. Outside the domain of grace, it soon degenerates into formalism and leads to ritualism. But like all sound laws, it exists both for the good of the individual person and for the common good of persons. Duly ordered liturgical worship sustains the People of God by maintaining, protecting and promoting the central reason for the existence of the Church, the adoration of the triune God.[197]

While there are more options and a more flexible pastoral approach as are evident today, this is no excuse for a cavalier attitude toward directives, rubrics and traditions. The anarchist approach to liturgy has caused great harm among the holy people of God. It cannot provide that *something more* which the Council Fathers called for, going beyond lawfulness and validity, because it has scorned the foundational structure of Christian worship. Those who are conversant with the liturgical law as their *guide to what should be done* in liturgy, have taught one a greater sympathy for those faithful families and individuals who worship God in churches where confusion and mistakes still reign.[198]

b. Responsibility and Competence

In an era when liturgical confusion and innovations linger, the New Code of Canon Law places a certain responsibility on parish clergy: the pastor is to see to it that the Most Holy Eucharist is the centre of the parish assembly of the faithful; he is to work to see that the Christian faithful are nourished through a devout celebration of the sacraments and especially that they frequently approach the sacrament of the Most Holy Eucharist and the sacrament of penance; he is likewise to endeavour that they are brought to the practice of family prayer as well as to a knowing and active participation in the sacred liturgy, which the pastor must supervise in his parish, under the authority of the diocesan bishop, being vigilant lest any abuses creep in.[199]

c. Faith and Culture

It is important to remember that while the Roman Rite is derived from Europe, this most widespread of the Catholic Rites is meant to be prudently inculturated. That delicate process is not necessarily the part to wild innovations, because true inculturation may also act as a brake on liturgical novelties that may have been imported by priests who have followed the latest trends in Europe and North America. This brings one to the inculturational aspects of the Eucharistic Celebration. Issues like the true cultural manner of giving sign of peace between men, between women, boys, girls, man and woman not his wife, between a boy and a girl who is not his sister or brother should bother serious liturgists.

Others include gestures and postures which are cultural to be admitted into the Church's liturgy, like the gesture for *mea culpa, mea culpa, mea maxima culpa* - through my fault, through my fault, through my greatest fault. Does striking the chest convey the true cultural way of expressing genuine sorrow, remorse and repentance? What cultural gesture expresses this sorrow best?

viii.   Conclusion

One of the concluding part of the priestly ordination Rite challenges especially the priests as follows: *accept from the holy people of God, the gifts to be offered to him. Know what you are doing; imitate the mystery you celebrate and model your life on the mystery of the Lord's cross.* The Church has got an inestimable value in the Eucharist, and she needs to guard it jealously. Let there be a conformity of understanding of the Eucharist with that of Christ, as expressed in the words and the rites of the liturgy.[200]

Abuses according to the Sacred Congregation on the Liturgy, contribute to the obscuring of the Catholic faith and doctrine concerning this wonderful sacrament. The Eucharist is so great a gift to tolerate ambiguity or depreciation. It belongs to the priests to make the Eucharist to continue to shine forth in all its radiant mystery and to transmit same faithfully and carefully to future generations.[201]

In an altogether particular manner, let everyone do all that is in their power to ensure that the Most Holy Sacrament of the Eucharist will be protected from any and every irreverence or distortion and that all abuses be thoroughly corrected. This is a most serious duty incumbent upon each and everyone, and all are bound to carry it out without any favouritism.[202]

Any Catholic, whether priest or deacon or lay member of Christ's faithful, has the right to lodge a complaint regarding a liturgical abuse to the diocesan Bishop or the competent Ordinary equivalent to him in law. or the Apostolic See.[203] Let all Christ's faithful participate in the Most Holy Eucharist as fully, consciously and actively as they can for each one should always remember that he is a servant of the Sacred Liturgy.[204]

Finally, every game has a rule. If one follows the rule, the game comes out beautifully well. The eucharistic liturgy is certainly much more than a mere game. Thus a higher level of obedience to the instructions is required. The beauty of the liturgical celebration depends to a large extent on intelligent adherence to the instructions. It pays always to obey reasonable laws like the liturgical laws. Availing oneself of the good opportunities like attending seminars on liturgy ensures self enrichment and updating in the new liturgical developments. There is a great need to make abundant use of the alternatives already approved to give variety to the celebrations for monotony kills interest, and variety they say is the spice of life.

CHAPTER FIVE:

Liturgical Preaching as Part of Christian Preaching

i.   Introduction

Within the varieties of Christian preaching is the liturgical preaching. Christian preaching as a form of public discourse has a number of different types or species which include: pre-evangelistic preaching, evangelisation, catechetical preaching or catechesis, preaching in church and liturgical preaching technically known as the homily *per se*.[205] We shall be dealing specifically with liturgical preaching or the homily. Our choice is informed by the fact that liturgical preaching seems to be a highly problematic area and the one most frequently discussed and debated.   Secondly, it is the only type of christian preaching listed above from which the laity are regularly excluded, although exceptions are allowed under certain circumstances as we shall see later.

Homily can best be understood as an enriched lively commentary on the Word of God. The church has always venerated the divine Scriptures just as she venerates the Body of the Lord, since from the table of both the Word of God and Body of Christ she unceasingly receives and offers to the faithful the bread of life.[206] What one finds common in the historical development of the homily is that it is more than any other form of Christian preaching.

It is the proclamation of God's wonderful works in the history of salvation, the mystery of Christ ever made present and active in us, especially in the celebration of the liturgy.[207] In all christian rites especially in the eucharistic celebration, the homily is related to the two tables of the Word of God and the Body of Christ and where it points the way to Christian involvement by communities and individuals.[208] In the full sense of the term, it is one of the ways of proclaiming the Word, a hermeneutic moment of actualisation and ecclesial interpretation, closely linked to the celebration of a christian assembly.[209]

ii.   Nature and Historical Development of Homily

The term *omilian poiein - homilian poiein* (Gk.) means familiar conversation, colloquy or informal discourse as can be seen in Lk.24:14; Acts 20:11; 1 Cor. 15:35. In Christian tradition, Ignatius of Antioch was seen urging Polycarp to preach against the heretics. Origen called his commentaries on the Scripture *Omilian*. In the fourth century, *Homilia* became a common term referring to all forms of preaching by the Church especially within the context of a liturgical celebration.[210] Corresponding to this Greek term are the Latin words *Tractatus* and *Sermo*. Augustine of Hyppo spoke of these informal discourses which the Greeks call *Homilias.[211]*

According to the witness of Justin Martyr in his first apology, while relating the homily to eucharistic celebration said, on the day called Sunday all gather in the same place, whether they live in the city or in the country. The memoirs of the apostles or the writings of the prophets are read for as long as time allowed. When the reader has finished, the president delivered a discourse (*logos*), urging and exhorting us to imitate these good examples.[212]

Against this background, it is possible to observe three outstanding elements as early as the middle of the second century as traditional regarding homily: the celebration of the Eucharist in the early christian communities was preceded by the liturgy of the Word. Secondly, the Word of God at eucharistic celebration is actualised in the homily. Thirdly, the *logos*, Word is delivered by the same person who presided over the entire celebration.[213]

iii.   Brief Historical Survey

a. Homily in Pre-Christian Era

Christian homily has a pre-historical antecedent. Preaching of homily reached an amazing development during the patristic era. Such homilies were deeply rooted in the Jewish synagogue worship form of preaching at the time of Jesus. The liturgy of the Word at this time consisted of reading of Torah, reading from the prophets, homily and prayer. The synagogue homily being a reflection of the entire biblical tradition, is completely original with respect to other cults. It is associated with the word and its special importance for these people, among whom it is constantly re-actualised in the face of new events and the demands of fidelity to the covenant.

Two texts gave us a very good idea of the function of the synagogue homily and summed up its history. Neh. 8:18 tells how Ezra read from the book of the law of God, interpreting and explaining its meaning so that everyone could understand the reading. Luke 4:21 recounts the words with which Jesus, in the synagogue at Nazareth, introduced his commentary on the reading of Is. 61:1-2.[214]

Synagogue worship concluded with prayers and psalms. It was a response to the word proclaimed and actualised, an expression of the dialogue between the God who revealed himself and the people which manifested its fidelity to him.[215]

b. Homily in Early Christian Era

Homily during the early christian era was dominated by Christ event. Actually, the verb *predicare* (Latin) and in Greek *kerussein/ evaggelixesthai* means to announce the coming of salvation, to solemnly proclaim that Jesus Christ is the Lord and Saviour. Homily must focus on the basic object of all christian proclamation namely, the Christ event of the Easter message, the Paschal Mystery which means in a nutshell, that Christ has died, Christ is risen, Christ will come again.

In the full sense of preaching homily, the christian preaching ought to be a proclamation of the Word. It is the ordinary way that leads to faith. Faith comes from what is heard, and what is heard comes through the word of Christ.[216]

Incidentally, Christ event is the interpretative key to all of salvation history and the new age that flows from his Passover. Every word of Jesus is filled with allusions to the ancient Scriptures. The apostles examined the Old Testament for words and events that are fulfilled in the mystery of Christ. The first christian communities expressed their faith awareness that Christ is present among them through the Word and sacraments of the Church.

Acts of the Apostles constantly provides evidence of the Apostle Paul as he conversed with his communities assembled in the name of the Lord. Traces of the early *haggadah* can be seen especially in the various Johannine texts, in first Corinthians and in first letter of Peter.[217]

c. Homily in the Patristic Era

The witness of Justin to the preaching of homily as an established liturgical practice would always remain credible reference point for subsequent liturgical tradition. between the second and third centuries, evidences already existed of the first documented christian homilies which include:

i. the homily of Pseudo-Hippolytus and

ii. the paschal homily of Melito of Sardis.[218]

   In these two texts, three clear steps within a homily are discernible:

   a. reading of the sacred text

   b. detailed explanation of what has been read

   c. contemplation of the mysteries in their realisation.[219]

The language and style of these two early texts carefully demonstrate a keen awareness of the signs of the times, shown in a strong desire to proclaim the things of God in human terms.[220]

d. Homily in the Fourth and Fifth Centuries

Fifth and fourth centuries have been aptly described as the golden age of the Fathers of the Church. The age featured great homily preachers as Origen and Cyprian. Others include Basil, John Chrysostom, Ambrose and Augustine. These displayed in their homilies, what homily in essence ought to be, namely an informal conversation by a pastor of souls with his people during a liturgical action based on the biblical texts presented by the liturgy.[221] The essential elements of a homily are derived from the fact that it is delivered during a liturgical action. These elements include:

i. **Topic**: this means that a specific aspect of christian mystery has to be named, which has to be shared and lived by the community.

ii. **Audience**: at this historical period, these were mainly uneducated people, including many catechumens who already believed but must be helped to a deeper understanding and assimilation. So the topic must be tailored to suit their level of comprehension and easy to be lived in practical life.

iii. **Speaker**: the speaker here namely the homilist was not one of the laity, whether more or less educated, but someone who has received the sacrament of orders which include, a bishop, presbyter or deacon whose very person serves to emphasise the essential connection between preaching and the christian celebration.[222]

The end of fourth century witnessed an extreme serious crisis in christian preaching. So seductive was the rhetoric in vogue in contemporary society that the homily was in danger of losing its simplicity and authenticity. But it was saved by the example of the two greatest homilists of the early church namely, St. John Chrysostom and St. Augustine. Their systematic reflections on christian preaching were profound and stimulating especially in their Treatises on the *Priesthood* and in *Book IV of De Doctrina Christiana* respectively.[223]

Toward the end of the patristic age in the West, two great popes also left for posterity, important homiletic models that would be very influential in the future: St. Leo the Great (+461). His magnificent sermons are full of theological and liturgical inspiration. St. Gregory the Great (+604). His simple and direct commentaries on Scripture are predominantly moral in their inspiration.[224]

e. Homily in the Middle Ages

Up until the middle ages, strong patristic influence on homily remained. However, christian preaching declined in the high middle ages. Selected texts from the Fathers, arranged according to the liturgical year in special collections (homilaries) were read. From the twelfth century on, preaching saw various revivals, but it became more and more detached from the liturgy. It was interpreted in succession by different oratorical genres which belonged more to the history of sacred oratory than to that of the genuine biblical-liturgical homily. The homily followed the historical vicissitudes of the rest of the liturgy until the liturgical reforms of the Second Vatican Council.

iv. Preparatory Grounds for the Liturgical Reforms of the Second Vatican Council on Homily

It has become the good wish of the Council Fathers of the Second Vatican that easy access to the sacred Scriptures should be provided for all the christian faithful[225] not only by merely reading the words of the sacred Scriptures but above all through exposure to biblically based homily.

The ground for the renewed vigour towards the abundant use of the Scriptures in the life of christians was softened especially by Pope Leo XIII in his encyclical letter, *Providentissimus Deus* (1833), by Pope Benedict XV in his letter *Spiritus Paraclitus* (1920), and by Pope Pius XII's *Divino Afflante Spiritu* (1943). Indeed, Sacred Scriptures are of paramount importance in the cele-bration of the liturgy especially in the eucharistic celebration.[226] For, it inspires the other prayers and songs of the eucharistic celebration, all the actions and signs of the liturgy derive their meaning from Scriptures.[227]

v. Homily according to the Reformed Liturgy of the Second Vatican Council

The statement prepared by the preparatory commission on the subject of the homily was generally well received. Those few Fathers who spoke referred generally to the obligatory nature of the homily which incidentally was insisted upon, and to the question of preaching syllabuses, which were not covered in *Sacrosanctum Concilium,* Document on the Sacred Liturgy, but taken up later in the *Instruction Inter Oecumenici* (1964)[228]

vi. Homily according to *Sacrosanctum Concilium* - Documents on the Liturgy

According to *SC*, Sacred Scripture is of the greatest importance in the celebration of the Liturgy. For from it are drawn the lessons which are read and which are explained in the homily.[229]

Second, the most suitable place for a (sermon) homily ought to be indicated in the rubrics, for the (sermon) homily is part of the liturgical action whenever the rite permits one. The primary source of the (sermon) homily, moreover, should be scripture and liturgy, for in them is found the proclamation of God's wonderful works in the history of salvation, the mystery of Christ ever made present and active in us, especially in the celebration of the liturgy.[230]

Third, by means of the homily, the mysteries of the faith and the guiding principles of the christian life are expounded from the sacred text (*ex textu sacro*) during the course of the liturgical year. The homily is strongly recommended since it forms part of the liturgy itself (*pars actionis liturgicae*). In fact, at those Masses which are celebrated on Sundays and holy-days of obligation, with the people assisting, it should not be omitted except for a serious reason.[231]

vii. Homily according to *Inter Oecumenici*

The Instruction *Inter Oecumenici* already cited above, deals with three questions that came up in the Council debate: obligatory nature of homily, preaching homily *ex textu sacro* and preaching syllabuses. Regarding the obligatory nature of homily, the Instruction says: there shall be a homily on Sundays and holy-days of obligation at all Masses.[232]

As regards preaching homily from the sacred text, the Instruction insists that a homily on the sacred text means an explanation, pertinent to the mystery celebrated and the special needs of the listeners, of some point in either the readings from sacred Scripture or in another text from the Ordinary or from the Proper of the day's Mass.[233]

As for the preaching syllabuses, the Instruction maintains that because the homily is part of the liturgy for the day, any syllabus proposed for preaching within the Mass during certain periods must keep intact the intimate connection with at least the principal seasons and feasts of the liturgical year, that is, with the mystery of redemption.[234]

viii. Homily according to *Editio Typica Altera* - Second Typical Edition of the Roman Missal of Paul VI, 1975

The introduction to the second typical edition of the 1975 Roman Missal of Pope Paul VI, gives an authoritative summary of all earlier documents that refer to the homily, adding a clarification thus: the homily should ordinarily be given by the priest celebrant.[235]

ix. Homily according to *Ordo Lectionum Missae*

The 1981 typical edition of the Order of readings of the Mass, recalls the most important teachings concerning the homily, describing it more briefly as ***part of the Liturgy of the Word***. But it adds some important directions thus: whether the homily explains the biblical word of God proclaimed in the readings or some other texts of the liturgy, it must always lead the community of the faithful to celebrate the Eucharist wholeheartedly, so that they may hold fast in their lives to what they have grasped by their faith.

From this living explanation, the word of God proclaimed in the readings and the Church's celebration of the day's liturgy will have greater impact. But this demands that the homily be truly the fruit of meditation, carefully prepared, neither too long nor too short, and suited to all those present, even children and the uneducated.[236]

x. Homily according to Post-Conciliar Documents of the Second Vatican Council

Besides these documents that deal directly with the liturgy, two post-Conciliar documents are worthy of citation. According to Pope Paul VI, a homily is a form of preaching which is specifically included in the celebration of the Eucharist from which it derives especial strength and force.[237] Furthermore, he sees the homily as a powerful and most suitable instrument of evangelisation.[238]

Pope John Paul II in 1979 in the apostolic exhortation describes the homily as catechesis given in the setting of the liturgy, especially in the eucharistic assembly. He invites his readers to respect and take advantage of its proper cadence, within the whole circle of the liturgical year.[239] Continuing his description of the homily, he states that the homily takes up again the journey of faith put forward by catechesis and brings it to its natural fulfilment. He further described homily as one of the benefits of the liturgical reforms.[240] These two documents insist that the homily should be carefully and appropriately prepared in accord with its special nature.

According to General Catechetical Directory the homily is the liturgical form of catechesis.[241] While stressing here that the various forms of the ministry of the Word are closely linked in reality, it distinguishes between evangelisation or missionary preaching, which is intended to arouse the first act of faith and catechesis, whose purpose is to re-awaken people to a conscious and active faith by means of suitable instruction. It notes that this catechesis also has a liturgical form.

xi.   Homily Among Other Forms of Christian Preaching

As earlier stated, the varied forms of Christian preaching include: pre-evangelistic preaching, evangelisation, catechetical preaching or catechesis, preaching in church and liturgical preaching.

i.   Pre-evangelistic preaching: would include all that came before the first proclamation of the Christian message, the preaching of true repentance by John the Baptist, and the preaching of Christ himself about the Kingdom of God which was in the midst of the people even as they listened to him.

ii.   Evangelisation (*kerugma*) is the first proclamation of the Christian message in order to arouse faith. Its content includes: Christ has died, he rose and will come again!

iii. Catechesis is the more systematic teaching aimed at believers in order to make their faith more active and conscious; stronger and better.

iv. Preaching in the church will refer to the preaching that takes place at other celebrations especially paraliturgicals and devotions in the church.

v. Homily is a special catechesis in the context of a liturgical action, closely connected with the word and rites. [242] These forms constitute the basic typology in christian preaching as is generally understood.

The Italian Bishops Conference in one of their important documents presented homily as follows: the homily is an integral part of the liturgical action from where it takes its movements and characteristics. Through the homily the designated minister proclaims, explains and pays tribute to the christian mystery being celebrated, so that the faithful might receive it intimately into their life and be disposed to bear witness to it in the world.

The homily derives its topics and themes primarily from sacred Scriptures and the liturgical texts of the Mass or the sacrament being celebrated. In the course of the liturgical year the homily illustrates the mysteries of faith and the norms for christian living, always with reference to Christ's paschal mystery. It takes into account the liturgical action that is going on, and it assumes a distinct tone: kerygmatic, doctrinal, moral or apologetic, depending on the particular needs of the faithful present.[243]

xii.   Homily as Part of Liturgical Action - *Pars Actionis Liturgicae*

As part of the liturgical action (*pars actionis liturgicae*) both at eucharistic liturgy and other christian rites, the homily is not simply an accessory or a digression, nor simply an explanation of the readings. It is indeed a certified part of christian celebration that actualises the word and fosters participation by the community, helping in its life what it has celebrated in the mystery.[244]

Within the liturgical celebration, the homily is thus located at the meeting point between the word proclaimed and Christ's sings, which converge to accomplish among the faithful the (*Mysterium fidei*) mystery of faith, the total event of human redemption. The event is prolonged and expressed in all the Church's liturgical actions, whether they are linked to temporal rhythms or to concrete situation in human life. In effect, the homily helps the assembly constantly to renew this faith experience. It gives the assembly a deep and living experience of that mysterious reality which the Church today has rediscovered in the words of Leo the Great: Our redeemer's visible presence has passed into the sacraments.[245]

Secondly, the homily cannot be isolated from the entire celebration in which it occurs and which it interprets. Its preparation and delivery must begin from the scripture readings. It must be co-ordinated with the admonitions, the penitential rite and the general intercession. It takes on the rhythms and features of an actual celebration and is able to draw inspiration from individual ritual or euchological elements or refer to them all in the context of a unitary and harmonious vision. A correct understanding of the homily, besides affecting its contents and methods, would also suggest that it should not be so long that it does not disrupt the rhythm of the liturgical action or compromise its overall effect.[246]

Furthermore, it belongs to the task of homily to be mystagogical in three senses:

i. it must be linked to a celebration as said above and situated at a specific moment between the word and the ritual. Along this line, it has to introduce the mystery celebrated and is itself the instrument and form of its accomplishment.

ii. It must be addressed to a christian community assembled for a specific liturgical experience, thus promoting its full and active participation.

iii. It has to bring out certain elements of the celebration as symbolic, capable of arousing faith and fostering christian experience.[247]

Still as part of liturgical action, the homily is to be given *ex textu sacro*, from a sacred text as already mentioned. The expression in effect means that a homily is primarily a commentary on the biblical readings of a particular liturgical celebration. By its very nature, it is linked to the word of God proclaimed within the christian assembly, and it is explained and actualised in this setting.

This does not apply only to the gospel, but also to the Old Testament readings, the letters of the apostles and the scriptural chants that accompany them. It must faithfully interpret the biblical texts in their exegetical sense and in their original context. It must show how the liturgical action becomes a new event and enriches the word itself with new meaning and power.[248]

The Lectionary of the Second Vatican Council is in many ways very important for a correct understanding of the homily of the Church today. According to the directives of *SC*. nr. 35.

i. today the reading of the word of God is more ample, more varied and more suitable.

ii. There are new criteria for selection and links between the readings, which should be known and properly used, which favour an overall inter-pretation.

iii. The constant presence of the Old Testament, besides offering pages filled with faith and life experiences, introduces the christian community to a historic-salvific vision inspired by the divine pedagogy and centred on the mystery of Christ, in which the christian life and the liturgical rites that are part of it take on a deeper meaning.

iv. The question of planned homiletic cycles, which was brought up again by some on the basis of *Inter oecumenici* nr. 55, needs to be dealt with using he thematic arrangement already found in the present order (semi-continuous reading, selection of passages that linked the liturgical year etc.), in view of a broader and more vital catechesis of a historical liturgical nature.

According to the introduction to the Missal of Paul VI, re-emphasising SC. 35, says that the homily should develop some point of the readings or of another text from the Ordinary or from the Proper of the Mass of the day, and take into account the mystery being celebrated and needs proper to the listeners.[249] In effect, the homily is in a special way an explanation of the readings, especially the gospel, but in special cases it can also present individual elements of the celebration (texts, gestures, signs). Through frequent use, these will perhaps remind the assembly to emphasise and actualise the biblical liturgical message in a christian celebration.

xiii.   Actualisation of the Purpose of Homily

One of the greatest bothering issues arising from homily today is its actualisation. Actualisation of the word has preoccupied many scholars, pastors and the laity. Liturgical experts are of the opinion that this problem touches on the purpose of homily and it is deeply rooted in the question of hermeneutics (principles of biblical interpretation). Preaching must be able to take the word in its original power and meaning and translate it into ever new expressions, courageously using it to confront the most dramatic aspects of our constantly changing culture and the crisis in which people find themselves today.

A possible principle is to go back to the same bible to discover actual paradigmatic model of the homily. A process of continual re-actualisation runs through the entire book according to a method that can provide one with exciting models.[250] One needs only to think of Deuteronomy with respect to Old Testament books that preceded it, to the developments in the books of Isaiah and Daniel. The word of God remains for ever, and in the rite it is presented again in relation to new events and cultic celebrations.[251]

xiv.   Ordinary Minister of Homily

Since the time of Justin down through the ages, it belongs to the clergy to preach at eucharistic celebrations.[252] The clergy include the church hierarchy in their order: the bishop, the presbyter-priest and the deacon. Normally the homily is reserved to the same minister who presides in continuity with his pastoral ministry within the community.

The close link between the two tables at the eucharistic celebration is also seen in the fact that the church entrusts the sacrament of the Word and the sacrament of the Eucharist, which form a single act of worship to the same minister. So in the West to say the least, preaching the homily at liturgical celebration has always been considered a presidential function. In the East there have been some important exceptions.

At eucharistic Concelebration however, the principle of division of labour could take place whereby the presidential function of delivering or preaching the homily is ceded to any of the Concelebrants. It is advisable in this case that the homilist reads the gospel too, so that the one who proclaims the gospel also breaks the Word for the people.

Secondly as he proclaims the gospel, he could emphasis the key words and phrases on which he would build up his homily. Again when the deacon assists at Mass, the same function of the president could be granted to the deacon which is the lower rank of the hierarchy.

xv.   Extra Ordinary Ministers of Homily

Certain questions arise today among scholars and some interested groups in the church like the female religious, lay theologians regarding the possibility of lay people to preach homily at eucharistic celebrations. As royal and prophetic people within their common priesthood, would the lay people preach at eucharistic celebration?

A very clear cut answer may not sufficiently solve the problem. Every christian is a priest, king and prophet but in varying degrees. The ministerial priesthood and baptismal priesthood ought to see each other in their proper perspective. The baptismal priesthood although subordinate to the ministerial or hierarchical priesthood, has to be in collaboration with the hierarchy. The sense of collaborative ministry comes into play here.

While maintaining the tradition of treating the preaching of homily exclusively as presidential, the sense of collaboration must not be entirely ruled out. In effect, there could be community preparation of the homily together with the president, contributions of specialists as their input in the preparation, personal witness from those helping in the preparations. Here also guided questions and answers could be allowed during the preparation. These contributions would enormously enrich the homily.

Through the power of delegation by appropriate authority, non clerical religious, lay people who preside at various rites like Sunday service without a priest, funerals, bible service etc. can also preach the homily. Even in exceptional case where the priest is unable to preach at liturgical celebrations for a very serious reason, non clerical religious, lay people could be asked to do this, with an appeal to the temporary or subsidiary nature of the role.

At a liturgical celebration where the priest presides and gives homily, non clerical religious, lay people could be asked to give some words of exhortation before the end of the celebration. This could be done with utmost discreet without having to give a second homily, a duplication which the liturgy abhors.

Furthermore, in several places, and on special occasions, an expert or a competent person, lay or religious could give an explanation. While this would be an exceptional case, it should not be ruled out altogether, especially nowadays when so many of the lay people are fairly competent even in theological and spiritual matters. According to D. Sartore, it seems essential that lay people be able to share with their pastors the responsibility for the word in a specific context, and that this collaboration maintains a secular character in keeping with the secular character of the laity themselves.[253]

Historically, lay preaching, in the general sense, not specifically the homily has been a practice in several different periods in the history of the church. There is evidence that some of this preaching was liturgical preaching. Lay preaching has been done by both women and men. However, women were excluded from lay preaching at times when lay men were still permitted to preach. Authorisation for lay preaching has been approached differently in various historical era.

The reasons for the prohibition of lay preaching at various times are complex and included political, social, cultural and ecclesiastical reasons as well as theological influences. At present, lay preaching is permitted under certain circumstances by church law. Lay preaching is growing as an accepted practice in some segments of the contemporary Roman Catholic Church like in Germany, Switzerland, Austria etc.[254]

The complexity of this history alone calls for humility and requires a genuine openness. No strong statement against lay preaching will hold up by itself against the overwhelming evidence of lay preaching in the history of the church. Lay preachers are so diverse as ordained preachers and cannot be stereotyped. Some have been influential in their communities and proclaimed a gospel that invited people to a deeper following of Jesus Christ. Others have had their own agenda and preached in ways that caused division and disharmony. In the midst of this kind of dialectics, the only salutary recommendation is to stick to what builds up the community and the over all good of the greatest majority of holy people of God.[255]

As far as the 1983 Code of Canon Law is concerned, the relevant Canons especially, Canons 759 and 230 para. 3, Canons 766 and 767 para. 1, among other things maintain that a homily at eucharistic celebrations by its very definition can only be preached by an ordained person. The ordinary minister of preaching at the Eucharist is the ordained celebrant, the presider. Other ordained ministers who are not the celebrant are considered extra ordinary ministers of preaching to a certain extent. A lay person could be authorised to preach on Sundays or holy days if there were serious reasons for omitting the homily.

If a lay person preaches at eucharistic celebration, that preaching is not considered a homily but rather another kind of preaching. These serious reasons include: in case of necessity and if it would be useful or advantageous. A lay person could be authorised to preach at children's eucharistic liturgies as contained in the *Directory for Masses with children*. A lay person could be authorised to preach at daily eucharistic celebrations since at these celebrations a homily is strongly *encouraged* but not *required*.

With regard to preaching at liturgical celebrations that are non eucharistic, there is some disagreement among Canonists about whether or not Canon 767 para. 1 applies to all of these liturgical celebrations or only to the Eucharist. However, there is general agreement among Canonists that lay persons can be authorised to preach in a number of different circumstances by either the bishop, the parish priest or rector of a rectory. For instance during Sunday celebrations in the absence of a priest; at certain rituals of blessing in which preaching is a part; during liturgies of the Word for catechumens, eucharistic exposition, funerals, non-sacramental penance services, celebrations of baptism, marriage and so on.[256]

The analysis made by the 1983 Code of Canon Law leaves rather room for further expansion of the opportunities for lay preaching, even liturgical preaching. Effective implementation for broadening the possibilities for lay preaching will require continued dialogue in a spirit of discernment. To do this well it will be important to insure that various interpretations of the law be brought into dialogue with the historical data and the theological concerns. Perhaps the most important aspect of this dialogue is that it takes seriously the experience of the good people of God in the pews.[257]

xvi.   Preaching Homily in the Third Millennium Church

Against the background of the renewed importance of the Scriptures in the liturgy by the Fathers of the Second Vatican Council in relation to what obtains in the local churches, one cannot but begin to wonder how faithful the homilists have dutifully carried out this special assignment. The liturgy prefers the term homily to sermon because of the radical difference between the two.

In the homily, the mysteries of faith and the norms of christian living are expounded. The homily draws from the sacred texts namely from the sacred scriptures read, the liturgical texts of the celebration or the liturgical season. While the homily is essentially a commentary on these sacred texts and applied to the level of the congregation, a sermon could speak rather on a more general terms and often moralises.

There are innumerable preachers today, especially since the upsurge of charismatic movements and renewals, many christian sects and evangelism, gospel preachers and healers, but there are very few homilists. Many of those who are meant to be preaching homilies seem to be carried away by the popular style of today's preaching hawkers.

Characteristics of such popular preaching methods include singing and clapping *ad nauseam* and dancing all of which often consume the entire time allotted to preaching the homily. Sometimes these actions substitute for the homily, thus suggesting emptiness and unpreparedness of the homilist. Virtue lies in the middle (*Virtus in medio stat)* applies very much in the art of delivering homilies in the liturgical celebration, especially at the eucharistic celebration.

xvii.   Issues involved in Preparing Homily Today

First and foremost, the passages have to be read at least three times by the homilist at the speed rate of slow, slower and slowest.

Second, some expert preachers recommend silent prayer over the texts for the unction of the Holy Spirit. This is where the collaborative input of com-munity preparation of homily shows itself most effectively.

Third, preliminary look at the readings. At this juncture, the homilist makes a preliminary approach and analysis of the three passages recognising the literary genre of the texts from the point of view of narrative, parable, hymn, exhortation etc. Attempt is further made to identify the key terms, the most important sentences, special difficulties involved in the texts etc.

The triple contexts of the texts have to be underscored: the biblical context of the text, a study of the liturgical text namely, the liturgical year, the choice of the texts and their intra-connections (connections among themselves), with the responsorial psalm and then the relationship of the biblical texts to the celebration and to the liturgical texts and rites. The third context is the identification of the community or the existential context.

In effect, the existential context recognises what crisis is touching the life of the community? What problems does the community feel most? What expectations does the community have from the celebration. In other words, who is being addressed? These three contexts could also constitute the vari-ous approaches one could decide to take in preaching.

The fourth stage in the preparation of homily demands the knowledge of the content of the homily. What themes are suggested by the readings and by the celebration? The central theme has to be identified and developed through reflection and actualisation in relation to the three contexts of theological, liturgical and existential contexts. It is recommended that a small unit of the central theme can be enriched through assimilation and resonance. More atten-tion is to be paid to a major theme or an element that can pull together the vari-ous aspects already mentioned.

Structurally, a homily should have a significant beginning, a series of deeper reflections in the middle as content and an appropriate conclusion. With regard to the content of homily, one needs to ask:

i.   How faithful is the homily to the biblical texts?

ii.   How is it related to the mystery being celebrated?

iii. How much attention does it pay to the community's life and present situation?

iv. What themes have been covered?

v. What main theme has been explored?

vi. What subjects come up too often in the church's homilies. Which are seldom treated? Which are habitually neglected? and why?

vii. From the point of view of actualisation, what areas of life do we normally mention? Family life, Personal life, Church life, Social life, Sociopolitical areas of life?

As a veritable means of communication, the homilist needs to undergo all these in order to pass on the message of salvation most efficiently.

xviii. Homily and Sign of the Cross

Because the homily is an integral part of the Eucharist, it should never begin or end with the sign of the Cross. This is one of the good achievements of the reformed liturgy of the Second Vatican Council which reduced the number of the signs of the Cross in the liturgy to the barest minimum.[258] Making the sign of the Cross, cuts the homily off as a separate section from the rest of the Eucharist, thus making it an entity in itself.

Even on this point, one can easily see the differences between the homily and the sermon. The latter always begins with the sign of the Cross and often this is followed by the announcing of the text on which the sermon is to be built.[259] This leads one to the subtle distinction between a homily and a sermon.

xix. Homily or Sermon

For most priests and liturgists trained before the liturgical reforms of the Second Vatican Council or a few years after it, a homily is no different from a sermon. Yet in the mind of the Church as we said earlier on, there is quite a big difference between the two.

A sermon is usually a lengthy well prepared discourse on a particular theme, which may or may not be part of the liturgy of the day or that is being celebrated.

Its style is highly oratorical and it is meant to impress the listeners. It is meant to move them even emotionally to either accept a particular truth or to set about practising it enthusiastically.

It usually has to be a fairly complete exposition of the theme and the ending particularly is exhortative and rousing. Most of the thinking is done by the preacher. He presents arguments in a fairly logical manner and often with the help of emotions including largely fear he drives home his message. The audience tends to follow, at times passively, and resolves to do what they have been exhorted to do.[260]

A homily on the other hand, aims at unfolding God's plan and action as depicted in the readings. Hence it is somewhat dispassionate and less oratorical or emotional. The homily places the broken Word before the people, leaving it to them to think out how they choose to respond. In that sense, it presumes a much more mature audience. It works best when it can be a proclamation, drawing the listener into the story and making it his or her story and thus evoking a response.

The homilist shares the Word with his people, leaving them always free to respond in the way and the measure in which they feel capable. The homilist thus invites more than exhorts or brow beats. Even the tone, the language and presentation, all change accordingly in a homily.

While there is room for sermons in the church's liturgical celebrations like at weddings, funerals, religious professions, ordinations etc, what seems to be asked for from the foregoing discussion on most Sundays and Holy-days of obligation is the homily. The homilist himself needs to have read the Word before and kept himself open to hear what God wishes to convey to His people through these readings.

Granted that the content of the homily should be based on the readings and take account of the mystery being celebrated, part of the homily can also deal with the various sections of the celebration like the parts of the eucharistic celebration: entrance rite, penitential rite etc, or even the prayers like the eucharistic prayer, the opening or concluding prayer.

The reason for this liturgical explanation of the contents of these sections as distinct from liturgical catechesis is because most of the people who attend the eucharistic celebration especially in the rural areas are ignorant of what the Eucharist is all about. Therefore, the topic of the homily could be anything within the celebration that could help the assembly to understand and celebrate the Eucharist better and more meaningfully.

xx.   Renewed Call for Authentic Preaching of Homily Today

Homily shares in the very mystery of Christ.[261] Although homily appears like familiar conversation, it is at the same time the Word of God. It is similar to Jesus Christ who appeared like an ordinary man, but he was at the same time the Son of God. Granted that by means of the homily, the mysteries of the faith and the guiding principles of the Christian life are expounded from the sacred texts during the course of the liturgical year the homily does not possess the universal value possessed by the Sacred Scriptures from where the homily draws, it is God's word on the level of the celebrating community.

The golden rule for the homilist is the following: If someone speaks, let it be as words of God (cf. 1 Pet. 4:11). For the listener, the golden rule is stated in what Paul said to the Thessalonians: You have welcomed the word not as a human word, but as what it really is, the Word of God (cf. 1 Thess. 2:13). Every homily should have this golden rule always in view.

Just as only the Spirit of God can transform the bread of the earth into the bread of heaven, thus only the grace of the Holy Spirit can transfigure familiar human words into true words of God. Hence, the principle of ancient exegesis formulated by Gregory the Wonder-Worker (+ circa 270) is valid for both the speaker and the listener: The same grace is needed for those who pronounce the prophecy (that is, the divine Word) as for those who hear it. And no one can understand the prophecy if the Spirit who prophesied does not grant him the understanding of his words.[262]

As the homily is closely related to the Word of God that is proclaimed, it is of paramount importance that it sustains the spiritual nourishment of the faithful. It is part of the liturgy and cannot be done without on flimsy grounds because it contains the necessary source of nutrition for the Christian life. Ideally, it consists of the systematic exposition of the scriptural readings or of some particular aspect of them, or of some other texts taken from the *Ordo* or the Proper of the Mass for the day, having regard for the mystery being celebrated or the special needs of those who hear it.[263]

In preaching homilies, prominence should be given to the biblical texts among other texts, because, the sacred Scriptures above all the texts used in the liturgical assembly enjoy a special dignity. In the readings, God speaks to his people, and Christ, present in his word, announces the good news of the gospel. By implication, it means that the liturgy of the Word ought to be celebrated with greatest possible reverence. Other readings from past or present, sacred or profane authors, may never be substituted for the word of God.

The liturgy of the word prepares for and leads into the liturgy of the Eucharist forming with it one act of worship. The two parts should not be celebrated separately at different times or in different places.[264]

With the Second Vatican Council, in its reforms on the liturgy, the role of the Bible has remarkably assumed a much higher role than it had in the pre-Second Vatican Council era. A lot of emphasis is now laid on the prominent role which the bible plays in the liturgical celebration.

Second, formerly the biblical texts were read in Latin which very few people well understood, and of course the preaching of the homily was in a foreign language to the people requiring the aid of an interpreter. But today, with the translation of the Bible into various languages and vernacular, the role of the Bible in the Liturgy has become more remarkable.

The importance of the homily in the liturgical celebration needs to be emphasised further. A very well proclaimed Word of God and well prepared homily nourish the faith of the members a great deal. It keeps the celebration alive. Such quality homilies are always appreciated. They are usually very challenging and never boring. The readings and the homilies are to be celebrated in the same manner as the words of consecration. They are as important as that. Just as the words of consecration cannot be uttered any how, the same applies to the readings and the homilies. The apostles in the early church refused to be distracted in order to have time for the Word and Prayer.[265]

The tendency today is to emphasise the celebration of the sacraments over and above the Word. This is the mentality which was inherited from the pre-

Second Vatican Council period. Today more than ever, the opportunity has been given to go back to the Word, to read, to love and to preach the Word of God. Every homily must speak of the life, passion, death and resurrection of Christ, namely, the paschal mystery. This is the core or the kernel of every homily. Otherwise, the homily is something else.

The Cross of Christ must not be found missing in homilies, especially against the background of a materialistic society that seems to be deviating from the Cross and going after a Cross-less Christ. The centrality of the paschal mystery of Christ must be sufficiently emphasised.

The homily is not first and foremost speaking about social problems but rather a commentary on the Word and the best commentary is from the bible itself, drawing instances from the Scriptures to corroborate the themes or the aspects of Christ's mystery that are being celebrated. That means that the ministers of the Word must make the bible their closest companion.

The Word of God, as it were, not only teaches, but convicts, heals and illumines. No wonder then what happens in some churches, after the celebration, the Word of God is enthroned on the Altar, and the Word then becomes really Emmanuel. The church has the tendency to lose many of her members as a result of this deficiency in handling the Word. This is because people come to the celebration and leave with spiritual malnutrition. They are rather over burdened with moribund liturgy.

But any where the Word of God is powerfully proclaimed and preached, (behind a powerful microphone or public address system), enriched with nourishing fruits of deep prayerful reflections, local idiomatic expressions, poetic forms, proverbs and wisdom tit-bits, with good liturgical and cultural music to help in digesting the Word and Signs, the situation is quite different. Such ceremonies are usually full and the christian life and culture boom.

Then in response, the people take up responsibilities to solve social problems, because they are now fully armed with Christ, and all these of course lead to reverence to the Word of God and the sacrament being celebrated. There is absolute need to make extra effort now to proclaim the Word of God with dignity, and make the crucified Christ central in all things.

xxi. At the Heart of the Homily lies the Paschal Mystery of Christ

At the heart of the homily is the paschal mystery of Christ. The image of the heart signifies the innermost core or centre of an organism, the starting point and terminus of the circulating blood. The heart is the vitalising centre without which life is impossible. As the principal organ, it supplies all areas of the body, even in their most minute parts, with the blood that is indispensable for life.[266]

The Paschal Mystery of Christ can be well understood in the broad and narrow senses as mentioned above. Secondly, it has a very close connection with the entirety of the christian mystery which is summarised in the Church's creed: the Holy Trinity, Creation, Fall, Redemption, Sanctification, Grace, Mariology, Sanctorals, Sacraments, Death, Judgement, Heaven, Hell. It remains the central and focal point of all that the church believes, celebrates and preaches.

The importance of the paschal mystery of Christ to the preaching of the homily cannot be over-emphasised. Actually, it is the nucleus, or better said, the vital axis of any homily that merits the name. It should be the nerve centre of all the preaching and all the catechesis derived from the life of worship, and should orient everything toward itself, for it is the central event in the history of redemption.[267]

xxii. Homily at Wedding Ceremonies

Homilies delivered during weddings should do well to emphasis the nature and the implications involved in the *communitas vitae et amoris* - community of life and love between the husband and wife as the ends of marriage. And in African culture particularly, the possibility of procreation of choice sexes and education of offspring constitute the burden of the homily. Secondly the aspect of service of communion for which the sacrament is known, namely the salvation of others should be very well developed.

Along side with the priesthood, marriage is understood as the second sacrament at the service of communion.[268] For in marriage, the couple dramatises the reality of the salvific love of Christ to the church. Husband and wife see themselves as reflective mirrors of the life long commitment of Christ to the Church. The couple puts into practice the unique sacrificial love that exists between Christ and the Church in a mutual bond.

It would be wrong for homilies at weddings to dwell too long on the personal qualities of the couple as if they are no longer in need of the grace of the sacrament. A homily with this kind of orientation leads to liturgical minimalism which pre-empties the mystery of the sacrament of marriage. Instead, the grace of the sacrament thus perfects the human love of the spouses, strengthens their indissoluble unity and sanctifies them on the way to eternal life.[269] Thus, the eucharistic celebration within which the wedding is celebrated and in which they share in the same Body and in the same Blood of Christ, they may form but one Body in Christ.[270]

xxiii. Homily at Funeral Masses

Very often funeral homilies degenerate into mere eulogies.Eulogies are forbidden.[271] The brief homily is not meant to be a eulogy or a panegyric in honour of the deceased. Often times, such homilies merely descend to sentimentality or triviality and sometimes rises to the heights of a solemn proclamation of beatification, if not an instant canonisation.

On the other hand, it would be difficult, if not callous, to exclude any reference to the deceased from the homily. Therefore, a pastoral common sense would modify a total ban of any comment on the life or character of the christian soul which the church in prayer is commending to the mercy of God.

Funeral homilies should never lose sight of three main points: entrusting the dead to the merciful Lord (*misericordia Dei*), the hope of the resurrection for the dead and the possibility of meeting again with the bereaved on the last day. Again most of the content and the main emphasis of the homily should consist of drawing out the revealed truths from the chosen readings, that, proclaiming the consoling but challenging facts of life and death, resurrection, judgement, purgatory and the hope of eternal life in heaven.

This is often a great opportunity for evangelisation, because, non-Christians apparently find the Catholic rites to be the most interesting and consoling of any funerals they attend. Here is one of those moments in the modern world when people are forced to face reality. Without being heavy handed, the homilist should seize such moments and use them for the glory of the risen Lord and the salvation of souls.[272]

Furthermore, in some places a eulogy could be given after the *Post Communion* Prayer and before the Rite of Final Commendation and Farewell. Here, a member or a friend of the family may speak in remembrance of the deceased. This seems the right time for such words, as long as they are brief, but it is not appropriate to intrude a eulogy into the Rite of Final Commendation and Farewell.[273]

xxiv. Preaching Homily in African Context

The rediscovery of the power of the Word of God since the reforms of the Second Vatican Council has made a tremendous impact on Roman Catholic celebrations in Africa. Before the reforms, the use of the Bible was associated with protestant worship, as recitation of the rosary was associated with the Roman Catholic worship.

But with the reforms of the Council, the love for the Word of God among Africans was predictably extended to the Jewish-Christian Scriptures in African Catholic celebrations.[274] For in Africa, the word is everything: it cuts and flays. It models and modulates. It perturbs and maddens. It heals and kills. It amplifies or lowers according to its force. It excites and calms souls.[275]

The celebration and sharing of the Word of God along the patterns of African rhetoric (audience participation, gestures, lyrical interventions) are acquired and practised all over Africa. Similarly, everyday concerns are integrated into the celebration of the liturgy (Word and Eucharist) in the form of bidding prayers rendered spontaneously. These crucial gains from the liturgical renewal of the Second Vatican Council are presupposed in the review of liturgical creativity in Africa.[276]

Africans believe strongly in the efficacy of Word. In Igbo culture, the oracles of the gods are sacred and binding. No one treats the oracles of the gods with levity of mind. The utterances of the gods are rather taken very serious. In the utterances of these agents are enshrined the morals, virtues and codes of conduct in relation to one another and in relation to God. One has no option when the gods have spoken through their culturally accredited agents. That boy calls you father....Yes, *Umuofia* has decided to kill him. The Oracle of the Hills and the Caves has pronounce it. They will take him (*Ikemefuna*) outside *Umuofia* as is the custom, and kill him there. But I want you to have nothing to do with it. He calls you his father.[277]

As a mark of deep respect and reverence, in the cultural set up, both the priest and the audience are both seated to listen to the utterances of the oracle. The assembly gathered to hear the oracles of the gods or to offer sacrifice to the Supreme God, endeavour to conduct themselves becomingly with the decorum proper to the gathering.

It appears unusual if not too casual to listen to God standing. Serious messages are received sitting down and very well composed. Such African comportment at worship will definitely enrich the celebration of the Word by the Afro-Christians a great deal. In the spirit of liturgical inculturation, the written word of God, and unwritten word of God though not to be taken on the same par stand to enrich one another in a mutual encounter.

The Word of God has universal application to all cultures. It is not restricted to a particular culture. It addresses and challenges all cultures. To deepen the cultural appreciation of the Word and eventual application, the Word of God needs to be read and interpreted in context. This calls for authentic African tools of biblical interpretation.

The Word has to be read with the eyes of the Africans and not with foreign spectacles; listened to with the ears of the Africans and not with foreign auditory aids; the Word has to be understood with the African mind and not with foreign mind sets; the Word has to be interpreted in respect to the African world-view and applied to her concrete different and challenging situations. Such applications will incorporate African major challenges like people's aspirations, desires, felt needs, problems, fears, and anxieties. An authentic African oriented interpretation and application of the Word of God, will be expected to take the people's culture and history into serious consideration.

xxv.   Varieties in Preaching Homily

Sometimes, the dialogue homily has been tried out in some places especially with children's Mass. In some places the dialogue is established between a lay person dialoguing with the celebrant. Where this is sufficiently well prepared, it can be a fruitful means of breaking God's word.

Similar to the dialogue homily are other means which are sometimes used with great benefit. These include audio-visuals where possible and even puppetry. These are of course specialised means and may not be available to everyone. Nevertheless, they should not be ruled out as possible methods or varieties in explaining God's Word.

If all this is to work out satisfactorily, it should be obvious that a lot of planning and careful attention to details is required. Most often, one gets into a kind of spiritual rut, presuming that there is only one way of approaching this point namely preaching the Word of God in the homily. The church does allow a lot of variety, but always with the good of the people in mind especially their active, conscious and full participation.

xxvi.   Practical Advice to Homilists Today

The first practical advice to homilists is to learn to keep it short. At eucharistic celebration, most people somehow seem to have an aversion for long-drawn preaching. Hence if the homilist could deal with just one point, tersely yet powerfully as a proclamation evoking a response, that would be acceptable and possibly fruitful also. Often homilists seem to feel that they must cover every possible angle of a given topic or issues raised in the readings.

In other words, they feel that they must do justice to the topic. That is not really necessary, since in the homily a lot of room must be left to the work of the Spirit. The more practical principle here would be: better a little that is understood and practised, than a lot, much of which would go undigested! [278]

Furthermore, the homily as earlier mentioned, must lead to some action, preferably within the Eucharist itself and then beyond. For instance, leading to a deeper self-surrender together with Jesus' self-offering, in other words to a greater participation. After all, the purpose of the entire liturgy of the Word is to rouse the assembly to a deeper participation in the self-giving of Jesus contained in the Liturgy of the Eucharist. However, this action should preferably come spontaneously, rather than be explicitly suggested or imposed by the preacher.

If this kind of response is genuinely and spontaneously produced within the Eucharist, most probably its effect will continue even during the rest of the day or week. Thus the celebrant will have fulfilled his job admirably, namely by facilitating each one's personal response to God's love, not only in ritual form, but also in actual life.

The homily then can be a very powerful tool in the hands of a zealous pastor seeking to help his flock to live their christian lives more energetically and meaningfully. However, it is worth repeating that he does this not by relying on his oratorical skills, but on the fact that he is in touch with the Spirit of God and speaks in His name.[279]

xxvii. Thirty Four Criteria for Assessing Good Homilies

i. Begin with a Captivating Introduction

A lot depends on the striking nature of the introduction of a homily. Today many homilists devise one strategy or the other. Some begin with a song, some with a short story, some with a quotation etc. One should be able to predict the quality of the homily even by the mere introduction of it. It does not need to be flat or dull. The introduction should be captivating, inspiring, vivid and relevant.

ii. Sufficiently Biblical

As mentioned earlier on, homily is a lively commentary on the liturgico-biblical texts particularly the scriptural aspect. Throwing biblical quotations indiscriminately without proper digestion and application is out of the question here. Often this art of preaching ends up in impressing the uninformed and drawing selfish attention to the preacher at the expense of Christ and his church. A sound homily in brief should display a good biblical content and background.

iii. Theological in Content

A sound homily must strive to be theological in content. Apart from being deeply grounded in Scriptures, it should strive to be a synthesis of some relevant patristic witness, magisterial pronouncements, contemporary input from theologians and individual preacher's personal appreciation of the theme. The ultimate conclusion has to lead to what the Church teaches. The practical contents must be easily applied in practical life of the people.

iv. Rooted in Sound Doctrine

Every homily must have its content based on one doctrine of the Church or another. The homily constitutes one of the privileged occasions to expound an aspect of the teachings of the Church.

v. Coherent and Well Organised

The homily should make sense, connected and organised. The ideas should not be disconnected otherwise it poses a problem of incomprehensibility.

vi. Characterised by Precision

The content of every homily must be exactly or accurately worded. The accuracy of wording a homily will enable the content and even the delivery to shine out very clearly. Precision enhances the quality of the homily and elevates the minds of the audience.

vii. Never Embarrass with Abuses or Insinuations

Every homily is first and foremost meant to edify and not to either demoralise or alienate anyone. It would be wrong for the content and manner of delivering homilies to degenerate into pouring abuses or insinuations of such on the holy people of God. The ordinary art of public address abhors embarrassing the audience, or running down any one or a social or religious system. The homily is not the proper forum to x-ray and criticise personalities, ideologies and socio-political agents or systems.

viii. A Display of Sufficient Mastery of the Theme or Topic

In delivering homilies, the homilist must convince his audience from the way he handles the issues or themes that he knows what he is saying. He must instil in his audience a reasonable degree of conviction in what he is saying. He needs to be sure of the topic and not guessing. He must display a certain appreciable level of authority both in content and in delivery of the homily.

ix. Devoid of Trivialities

Bearing in mind that liturgical celebration is a public worship as opposed to being some private or personal affair, issues of little consequence should not be allowed into the homily. Such commonplace issues lead to liturgical minimalism and very strange to the classical liturgy of the Roman Rite. Issues in the liturgy must be dignified to correspond to the dignity of the mystery of salvation being celebrated.

x. Concrete and Vivid Illustrations

Painting clear pictures and creating practical examples go a long way to enhance the quality of homily. Illustrations however, should be done with caution and moderation, so that the audience does not miss the true message by clinging to examples.

xi. Offer Guiding Principles to Good Christian living

Homily ought to be rich in content such that it offers the audience a means of improving the quality of their christian life. The content must be very challenging to the audience so that they feel they have got something for the upliftment of their life as christians.

xii. Tailored to Meet the Needs of an Audience

The quality of the homily both in content and delivery must take into consideration the level of the congregation. It would be wrong to deliver a homily that is above the level of intelligence of the people. Like the good shepherd, the homilist must be able to size up the ability of the audience and thus develop the homily to suit their level of understanding.

xiii. Have a Tinge of Newness to Familiar Topics

A homily must have something new each time to put across to the audience and this newness must be self-evident. Even as the homilist repeats the same homily during the three year cycle for Sundays and two year cycle for Weekdays, it would not be proper to repeat oneself each time verbatim. The homily must have some slight flavour or traces of newness, from extra research, new examples or illustrations and different styles of delivery.

xiv. Lively and Inspiring

Perhaps this deals more with the manner of delivery. No one enjoys a dull and uninspiring homily. A situation where the church wardens are very busy going around the congregation and waking them up is already a small index of a big whole. The homilist ought to re-assess himself in the light of the manner of delivering homily. A number of things could be responsible for this failure: sheer lack of preparation, the posture at delivering homily, reading a long text, the manner of speaking, using bed-room or conversational voice instead of the preacher's voice etc.

xv. Address Current Human Life Experiences

As part of speaking to the audience at their level belongs the fact of addressing current human life experiences. The audience usually has wrapped attention when the homily addresses their concrete and current life experiences. But if it falls short of this, the audience very easily tunes off and one is left with mere body presence with their minds completely elsewhere or at best, they resort to continue their sleep.

xvi. Utilise Concrete Circumstances of Current Living

A good homily must be able to address and use concrete circumstances of current living to corroborate itself. Abstract circumstances rather obscure the message of the homily which makes applicability rather impossible. It has to be well adapted to the group both linguistically and intellectually.

xvii. Delivered in a Polished Language

Liturgy abhors vulgar or foul language. Use of raw languages, crude expressions, unrefined idioms, street and market-place slangs and clichés not only minimise the quality of a homily but can also militate against the entire homily. In delivering homilies such unpolished languages should be shown the way out. The homily could still stand well without them.

xviii. Sequenced Logical Message

The message of the homily should be orderly arranged to facilitate comprehensibility and remembrance. The logical message needs to flow in a simple sequence. This should not be presumed in preparing and delivering homily. If the message is so scattered, it impairs applicability to even practical life.

xix. Ability to Stimulate Behaviour Modification

One of the necessary features of a good homily is the ability to challenge the audience into decision and change. Flat homilies can hardly do this. When people have been fed with the fruits of the Word in the homily, they are compelled to model their life according to the Word, which most often presuppose a new line of action as evidence of changed life pattern.

xx. The Preacher Must Be A Model of What He Preaches

The eternal verity which states that actions speak louder than words has never been faulted by anyone or any age. The preacher who preaches about the Cross must be the seen to visit and listen with keen interest to patients with chronic and incurable diseases. The homilist who spent time to preach charity must be seen to part with ease the reasonable creature comforts around him. The preacher must practice what he preaches.

xxi. Reasonably Short

A brief but captivating homily is preferred to a long and boring homily. 15-20 minutes on Sunday would be ideal. If after fifteen minutes one is unable to hit the point, something is wrong somewhere. 5-8 minutes on weekdays would also be recommended. A homily must never be too lengthy. As a matter of principle, it is better a point in a short time than many points long over drawn.

A well prepared and written homily delivered in a short space of time would be edifying. A written homily does not automatically mean reading it out verbatim. The presence of a written text has a tremendous psychological effect on some homilists in general. It instils confidence both on the homilist and the audience. Above all in a written homily, one could reasonably say a lot within a given time. Written homily is a discipline in its own category.

Sometimes although, the sight of a written homily puts some members of the assembly off, as that could indicate to them an academic paper about to be read or the forgetting tendency of the preacher. In that case, if he does not remember what he is to preach, how would he expect the people to remember what he has preached.

xxii. In Tune With The Liturgical Season or Occasion

As an integral part of the liturgical celebration, the homily would have to underscore the liturgical season or the occasion. The liturgical season and the occasion should be reflected reasonably in the homily. The liturgical seasons include, Advent, Christmastide, Short Ordinary Time or Pre-Lenten Season, Lent, Eastertide until Pentecost, Long Ordinary Time ending with the Solemnity of Christ the King of the Universe. Liturgical occasions include, Baptism, Confirmation, Ordinations, Religious Professions, Weddings, Funeral etc. the homily on such occasions has to throw some reasonable light on the seasons and makes a clear connection between the season or occasion with the on going celebration.

xxiii. Use of Appropriate Stories

Spiritual lessons could be made permanently memorable through appropriate stories. Stories like proverbs, idioms and local linguistic expressions have a very clear and distinct way of making a homily down to earth, easily comprehensible and memorable. Prudent use of relevant stories could be of immense use in internalising the spiritual lessons drawn from homilies.

xxiv. Make Them Laugh But Make Them Think

Use of relevant penetrating and thought provoking humour has a double task of making the audience to laugh but makes them at the same time to think. Ordinarily, humour is one way of releasing inner tensions and resentments. Speech makers often express difficult ideas humorously. However, without reducing the entire homily to an amusement spree, judicious use of humour could serve as one means of making the audience laugh and also think. Under the spell of humour the homilist could tactfully, plant, provoke and uplift the minds of the assembly to the higher level of reasoning. To end up only with excitement or laughter would be a total failure on the part of the homily.

xxv. Use of Anecdotes

Short stories make the homily picturesque. Straight forward and uncomplicated stories make the homily very vivid and striking. Anecdotes have to be used also with prudence so that the aim of illustrating the idea raised in the homily will not be lost in the stories. They should be edifying, interesting and relevant.

xxvi. Effective Use of Public Address System

The essence of public address system is to facilitate communication. Public speakers like homilists should know how to use the system especially by speaking into it. A functional public address system ranks among the prominent assets in the homily. To be heard clearly and distinctly by everyone enhances active participation not only in the homily but also in the entire liturgical celebration. A well prepared homily but poorly communicated should be considered a huge waste. Above all, it irritates and alienates the audience as it frustrates the homilist. A poor public address system is capable of ruining the entire homily.

xxvii. Jokes

Jokes like anecdotes could be very useful in delivering homily. But when they become dry and expensive, they mar and make the homily sour. Homilies should be devoid of dry and expensive jokes. Above all jokes should not be over done.

xxviii. Exclude Repetitions

Homily becomes nauseating when it is over burdened with repetitions, repeated flat jokes and endless repeated choruses. Now and again, a homilist could repeat himself for the sake of emphasis otherwise, repetitions should be avoided as much as possible. They diminish the quality of a homily. A homily with intermittent jokes and hymns reasonably timed and not over dramatised comes out well always.

xxix. Expose the Ills of the Time or Society

As a lively commentary on the Word of God which is used to teach or to instruct, advice or admonish and correct errors, the application of the homily should also be courageous in not only exposing the ills of the time or society but should indicate some salutary path to remedy. As already highlighted above, a homily should not be abusive, confrontational or partisan in approach. It must steer the course of truth in charity so that one does not lose both the dirty water and the child. A homily should always indicate signs of hope, evidence of courage to begin again and rays of light at the end of the dark tunnel.

xxx. Hand Down the Eternal Truth of the Gospel

The content of the homily could be no other than the eternal truth of the Word of God to be applied to human conditions for the total transformation, sanctification, edification and the glorification of God. To hand down the truth of the gospel is a special entrustment given to the homilist. He is then compelled to hand down this eternal truth without fear or favour. That does not exclude the use of prudence, initiative and common sense in fulfilling this unique salvific function.

xxxi. Based on the Paschal Mystery of Christ

The paschal mystery of Christ constitutes the burden of every homily. By paschal mystery of Christ in a nut shell, as well as the paschal mystery of Christ in a broad sense. As mentioned earlier, every homily should highlight an aspect of these mysteries of Christ. Every homily in other words must be Christ's-mystery-centred.

xxxii. Coherent Message of the Readings

Homily should strive to make a clear unit and coherent synthesis of the three readings of Sundays or two readings of the Weekday. Thus, the homily achieves a coherent message of the readings. It makes it easier for the audience to follow and retain for further meditation and application in practical life.

xxxiii. Concluded with the Major Highlights

The points raised at homily should not be left without a proper conclusion. A homily has to end with well concluded major highlights. It makes for a tidy job and easy to remember the various important issues raised in the homily.

xxxiv. Preach this Homily to Oneself

The effectiveness of a homily begins with preaching the homily first to oneself. It is very much recommended that one does this before the Blessed Sacrament only after then can one go out to preach it to others.[280]

xxviii. Conclusion

Homily is an integral part of the liturgical celebration. It is quite different from sermon. A homily can draw from the biblical texts, readings, responsorial psalms, alleluia verse, the liturgical season and the euchological formulary of the celebration. A sound homily has the tremendous effect of building up the spiritual and physical fortifications of the members of the church. The members feel satisfactorily nourished by a well prepared and masterly delivered homily.

With its soothing traits, the church is able to withstand all her trials and tribulations. With its challenging tendency, the church braces for action in the continuous christian warfare and ultimately leading to the perfect praise of God in their lives.

It is a liturgical act. It is characterised by exposition of the text with little background, exhortation and challenges, and must have bearing with realities of the life of the audience. Its effect must spill over to the extra liturgical arena and constitute a thematic agendum in the lifestyle of the assembly. A fire brand homily is both formative and informative, hopeful and optimistic and above all positive to life and its vicissitudes. It is essentially a means of communication.

If there is any thing a homily is not, it is not an occasion or forum for venting one's personal anger, a public x-ray of any person or system, or being arrogant in speech (cf. Eph. 4:29-32). Even in correcting errors or rebuking, the nature of the homily still demands prudence and edifying methodology with the ultimate intention of winning back souls for the Lord.

The best of homilies is the one which is first preached to oneself. A well written homily still remains the ideal for the numerous advantages it has. A written homily facilitates a good take-off and guarantees a safe landing. It curbs the irritating practice of endless repetitions. It is usually precise, *ad rem,* and gives the psychological satisfaction of being prepared and being very well in control of the theme.

Being written does not necessarily mean that it has to be delivered by reading the text word. A written homily convinces the homilist and the audience of exercising a serious, formal and public function, and not a casual speech or mere conversation.

Best of homilies is also usually the fruit of many hours of prayer, study, reflections on the text and dexterity in application. Part of good homily lies in the art of delivery. First, it has to be delivered with very clear and distinct voice, popularly referred to as the preachers voice, and not with a bed room voice. Proper use of public address system is equally an added advantage. The same applies to the proper use of local expressions, idioms, proverbs,[281] didactic stories, literary genre and prudent use of tortoise stories[282] especially for children.

The proper use of the voice is important in the context of preaching a homily. But there is equally a need to develop the more subtle art of the liturgical use of the voice. Affectation should be avoided, but skills such as dignity of expression and giving value to the meaning and sense of words are essential, not only for communication, but for the distinctive proclamation of public speech.[283]

The words of Karl Rahner are aptly applicable at this juncture. While underscoring the difficulty of the preaching task, he urges preachers to exercise existential imagination so that they can preach to the non-believers among us, moving them to conversion and fuller freedom. Preachers need to maintain a realistic yet creative approach to their task, reflecting the struggle in which we are all engaged in while at the same time offering hope in a world tempted to despair. God will redeem and liberate us only if we take the risk of preaching the message of God with strength and conviction. Indeed, it is only when the message of the living God is preached in the churches with all the power of the Spirit will the impression disappear that the church is merely an odd relic from the age of a society doomed to decline.[284]

The right and the need of the People of God to hear the Word of God preached well and effectively are paramount. The Word of God, the message of the living God can be preached effectively by both ordained and lay preachers, who share a common baptism and mandate for preaching. Together they can bring vitality and enthusiasm for the preaching ministry, which will feed the good People of God in abundance, not unlike the miraculous event of the loaves and fishes, which at first was not enough to feed the people who were famished, and then, there was such an abundance that could be used to feed others.[285]

The common baptism and mandate as basis to preach homily by the ordained ministers and lay preachers ought to be understood always in its proper perspective. The varying degree inherent in this task for both the ordained ministers and lay preachers as well as the subordinate and proper authorisation required by lay preachers should always be kept in view. Lay preachers have to exercise this function always with recourse to the prescribed provisions as contained both in the 1983 Code and liturgical laws.

The Word of God is preached effectively when the assembly gathered, both preacher and listeners, become actively involved in the preaching act as participants; when the Word proclaimed and received interpret the lives and experiences of the preacher and listeners in the light of God's saving act in Christ. Preaching is effective when the gathered assembly is transformed, when they begin to see with new vision, hear with new acuity, and hope in new possibilities for themselves, the community, the world; when the Word and works of justice, healing and reconciliation are proclaimed unceasingly.

A homily properly handled would always be appreciated. It must never degenerate into what happened in the high middle ages, when vigour, simplicity and authenticity of the homily was lost to documentation. Today a well prepared and masterly delivered homily still remains to the worshipping community a boom and a boon.

GENERAL CONCLUSION

What the diviners in African Traditional Religion stand for in their community could serve as a veritable legacy worthy of emulation by the church. A pastor of souls who is remarkable for having some listening ears to the cries and woes of his people remains an invaluable asset to the people. His ability to be very close to the divine instils even more unconditional confidence and therapy to his clients. His dexterity in performing the redressive rituals after due consultation with the divine brings the client the necessary tranquillity and ultimate healing.

Imperfect as the ATR diviners may be, their functional utility in the community cannot be overemphasised. They not only provide hope to the hopeless, but also remain a credible link between the people and their God.

Today more than ever, the awareness of the profound nature of social justice-oriented liturgical spirituality needs to be further intensified especially the potentials such an awareness holds for contemporary times. Liturgical spirituality has to be seen as a school of discipleship, that is, the source of direction for the Christian life, for the liturgy expresses the reality of the christian life, yet it is also the font from which the Church draws the strength necessary to live the paschal mystery in the modern world.

In order to enhance liturgical spirituality that is justice oriented, there is need to form the baptised faithful through a model of Church - centred faith formation that integrates liturgy, justice, and catechesis. The process of bringing people to see the relationship between the Church's liturgical life and the work of justice would be greatly enhanced by understanding catechesis as an essential element in a more comprehensive approach to faith formation.

The world today is in dire need of peace, unity and justice. These have constantly eluded the world today. These values could be re-cultivated by recourse to the sacrament of unity, peace and justice namely, the Eucharist.

In the eucharistic mandate, the church is expected to complete the work of Christ on earth by continuing to carry on the mission which Christ began while he was on earth. This includes the mission of announcing the good news to the poor, freedom to captives and joy to mourners.

Jesus sends the Holy Spirit to believers to make them his ecclesial body in space and time and to inspire them to carry out this mission. Jesus, through his members, brings the fullness of grace to men and women down through the ages and ultimately through the consummation of creation on the last Day. A significant factor in completing Jesus' work is struggling for social justice, even as it implies love, humility and other virtuous attitudes and activities.

Ite Missa est at the end of every eucharistic celebration is not only a statement about what may have occurred personally in the course of the celebration just completed, it is also the beginning of a mission, or the renewal of a mission, to seek that social justice which corresponds to God's reign on earth as in heaven. As the participants take their exit, they go to embrace and tackle social justice issues in the larger society.

The mystery of the Eucharist is so great for anyone to permit himself to treat it according to his own whims, so that its sacredness and its universal ordering would be obscured.[286] For arbitrary actions are not conducive to true renewal. The result is uncertainty in matters of doctrine, perplexity and scandal on the part of the people of God and almost as a necessary consequence, vigorous opposition all of which greatly confuse and sadden many of Christ's faithful in this age of ours when Christian life is often particularly difficult on account of the inroads of secularisation as well.[287]

For the homily to retain its pride of place in simplicity and authenticity, a return to the christian and patristic eras would seem very much recommended. The Christ's event remains an irreplaceable hallmark of christian preaching. A systematic reflection on christian preaching as exemplified in St. John Chrysostom and St. Augustine still serves as ideal for the modern homily in the third Millennium church. A sound homily must not lose sight of the topic, the audience and the preacher who has to down-load the biblical texts and package them properly for easy consumption within the liturgical celebration by the assembly against the backdrop of fast and modern communicational facilities and challenges.

As often as possible today's preachers of homily should have recourse to the preaching models of Christ and the two great popes: St. Pope Leo the Great and St. Pope Gregory the Great. Their insistence on drawing out the deep theological, liturgical and moral inspiration in every homily well applicable to the existential situations in practical life can never be over stressed.

NOTES

General Introduction:

1 Pope Pius X11, *Mediator Dei*, *AAS* 39 (1947) 528-9.

2 A. J. Chupungco, Editor, *Handbook For Liturgical Studies, Introduction to the Liturgy, A Definition of Liturgy*, A Pueblo Book, The Liturgical Press, Collegeville Minnesota, 1997, p.4.

3 *Sacrosanctum Concilium - Document on the Sacred Liturgy, hence forth SC.* nr. 7.

4 Cf. A. J. Chupungco, *Introduction to the Liturgy*, p.4 - 5.

5 Cf. SC. nr. 9.

6 Cf. *SC.* nr. 10.

7 Cf. *SC.*, nr. 14.

8 Cf. *SC.*, 37-40.

9 Cf. *SC.*, nr. 21.

10 Cf. *SC.* nr. 48.

11 Cf. *SC.* nr. 37.

12 Cf. E. E. Uzukwu, *Worship as Body Language, Introduction to Christian Worship*: *An African Orientation*, A Pueblo Book, The Liturgical Press, Collegeville, Minnesota, 1997, p. 267.

13 Cf. *SC.* 21 and 48.

14 Cf. A. J. Chupungco, *Introduction to the Liturgy*, p. 7.

15 Cf. *Ibid.*

16 Cf. *Ibid.*

17 Excellence in all scores includes: in preparation for it, in attendance meaning to be well attended, made to be attractive, made to make difference so that those who attend will thank their stars and those who were absent would have cause to regret for what they have missed for not being there etc. But if it makes no difference to the people, the aim is certainly defeated.

18 Jesus on the Cross forgave the persecutors because they do not know what they do. Today's oppressors incidentally fully know what they are doing. That makes forgiveness today somewhat problematic. But when one realises that forgiveness is a gift of God - *per donare* in Italian, forgive - *to give before* that makes a world of difference. All the same, humanly speaking, there can be no true reconciliation without a proper redress. If one says he is sorry, one must be able to call the ills he or she is sorry for by their names, and do something to show remorse and redress the action. Restitution for instance is the hallmark of redressing stealing or robbery.

Chapter One: Structures of Rituals: Rules and Creativity:

[19] Cf. *SC*. nr. 38.

[20] AA. VV., *Liturgiede l'Eglise particuliere et Liturgie del'Eglise universelle,, Conference Saint Serge, XXIIe Semaine d'Etudes liturgiques, Paris, 30 – 3 July1975, Edizione Liturgiche, 1976.Paris, quoted by* E. Uzukwu,, *Worship as Body Language, p. 265.*

[21] This chapter is the full text of the Conference Paper presented by me at the Annual International Conference organised in partnership between the Katholieke Universiteit Leuven, *Omnes Gentes* and *Missio* Belgium, with the Theme: ***Rituals For Life***, October 28-30, 2004. An extract of this paper is hoped along with other papers of the conference in the University's Journal: Questions Liturgiques- QL in 2005.

[22] Cf. P. Oliviero and T. Orel, *L' Experience Rituel, Recherches de Science Religieuse* 78/ 3:1990, 329-72 esp. 331-4 quoted in: Elochukwu E Uzukwu, *Worship As Body Language,* p. 42.

[23] Victor Turner, *The Forest of Symbols, Aspects of Ndembu Ritual,* Corneil University Press, Ithaca and London, 1991, p.19.

[24] Cf. Elochukwu E Uzukwu, *Worship As Body Language,* p. 41.

[25] Cf. Victor Turner, *The Forest of Symbols, Aspects of Ndembu Ritual,* p. 25ff.

[26] Cf. *Ibid.*, p. 26.

[27] Cf. *Ibid.*, p. 50-57.

[28] Cf. O. Imasogie, *African Traditional Religion,* University Press Ltd., Ibadan, 1985, p. 67.

[29] Cf. J. S. Mbiti, *African Religions and Philosophy,* Heinemann Educational Books, London, 1985, p. 172ff.

[30] Cf. *Ibid.*

[31] Cf. G. Parrinder, *African Traditional Religion,* Sheldon Press, London, 1961, pp. 120-121.

[32] Telepathy is described as a thought transferred from one mind to another without being conveyed by any known physical means.

[33] Cf. A. Shorter, *African Culture and the Christian Church,* Geoffrey Chapman, London, 1973, p.137. This is not only the ability of the diviners but also of some spiritual people who pray a lot and try to be close to God

[34] Cf. J. S. Mbiti, *Concepts of God in Africa,* SPCK, London, 1982, pp. 223-224.

[35] Cf. E. Ikenga Metuh, *Comparative Studies of African Traditional Religion,* Imico Publishers.....(Nigeria), 1987, p.230.

[36] Cf. *Ibid.,* p. 27.

[37] Cf. Elochukwu E Uzukwu, *Worship As Body Language,* p. 53.

[38] Cf. *Ibid,* p. 54.

[39] Cf. *SC.,* nr. 37; *Decree on Ecumenism* nr.16.

40 Cf. *SC.* nr.38.

41 Cf. Elochukwu E. Uzukwu, *Liturgy Truly Christian Truly African*, p.21-22.

42 Cf. E. E. Uzukwu, *Worship As Body Language*, p. 302.

43 Cf. *Nostra Aetate, On the Relation of the Church to Non-Christian Religions*, (Henceforth *AE*) nr. 2.

44 Anyi ayoo gi, 2ice, Ezi Chukwu 2ice, nabataya, were ya gozie ya meekwa ya Nna ka odi nma, tosi n'iga anara ya with gesticulations by young girls.

45 cf. J. Cardinal Tomko, *Auditio* in: Special Assembly for Africa of the Synod of Bishops, Vatican, 10th April - 8th May, 1994, p. 10.

46 Cf. *Bulletin* 11-14 .04. 1994-7 *of the Special Assembly for Africa of the Synod of Bishops*, Vatican, 10th. April - 8th. May, 1994.

47 Cf. Elochukwu E Uzukwu, *Worship As Body Language*, pp.265-272ff.

48 Cf. *Ibid., Worship as Body Language,.....* p. 271-272. From pp. 265-316, Uzukwu discusses extensively the emergent forms liturgical creativity has taken place in Africa.

Chapter Two: *Spiritus et Sponsa*: The Spirit and The Bride:

49 Cf. Pope John Paul II, *Apostolic Letter, Spiritus et Sponsa - The Spirit and the Bride*, On the 40th Anniversary of the Constitution on the Sacred Liturgy, *Sacrosanctum Concilium*, Dec. 4, 2003, nr.1.

50 Cf. *Ibid.*, nr. 2. Cf. also,

51 Cf. *Ibid.*, nrr. 3-4.

52 Cf. *Ibid.*, nr. 3.

53 Cf. *Ibid.*, nr. 6.

54 Cf. *Ibid.*, nr 7.

55 Cf. *Ibid.*, nr. 8.

56 Cf. *Ibid.*, nr. 9.

57 Cf. *Ibid.*, nr. 10.

58 Cf. *Ibid.*, nr. 11.

59 Cf. *Ibid.*, nr. 12.

60 Cf. *Ibid.*, nr 13.

61 Cf. *Ibid.*, nr. 16.

62 Cf. Pope Pius XII, *Mediator Dei*, AAS 39(1947), pp. 547-572.

63 Cf. Jesus Castellano Cervera, O.C.D., *Liturgy and Spirituality*, in: Anscar J. Chupungco, O.S.B., (editor), *Handbook For Liturgical Studies*, vol. 2, *Fundamental Liturgy*, A Pueblo Book, The Liturgical Press, Collegeville Minnesota, 1998, p. 45. There are other scores of authentic sources dealing with the harmonious relationship between Liturgy

and Spirituality. These include: *Liturgy As A Formative Experience*, in: *Studies in Formative Spirituality*, 3 (1982); *Liturgie et spiritualite*, La *Maison Dieu* 154 (1983); *Liturgia: Spiritualita nella Chiesa, RL* 4 (1986) etc., (henceforth *MD*).

64 Cf. *SC*. nr. 14.

65 Cf. SC. nr. 7.

66 Cf. *The Catechism of the Catholic Church*, (Henceforth *CCC*), English Translation for Africa, Paulines/Libreria Editrice Vaticana,1994, nrr. 1070, cf. also nrr 1077-83, 1084-90, 1091-109.

67 Cf. *Dogmatic Constitution on the Church, Lumen Gentium* (henceforth *LG*) nrr. 40-42.

68 Cf. Jesus Castellano Cervera, *Liturgy and Spirituality*, p. 49.

69 Cf. *Ibid.*, p. 50.

70 Cf. *The principle of The Rule of St. Benedict*, chapter 19.

71 Cf. *The Golden Principle of the Easter Collect for Neophytes*, cf. also *SC*. 10 and 11.

72 Cf. *SC*. nrr. 10, 12.

73 Cf. *SC*. nr. 11.

74 Cf. *SC*. nr. 12.

75 Cf. *SC*. nr. 13.

76 Cf. *SC*. nr. 10.

77 Cf. *Ibid.*

78 Cf. *LG*. nrr. 10 and 11.

79 Cf. *LG*. nr. 34.

80 Cf. Paul VI, *Apostolic Constitution, Laudis canticum*, Jan. 11th, 1970, nr. 8.

81 Cf. *CCC*. nr. 1070.

82 Cf. *Ibid.*, nr. 1091.

83 Cf. *Ibid.*, nr. 1098.

84 Cf. *SC*. nr. 7.

85 Cf. Rom. 8:26-27.

86 Cf. Jesus Castellano Cervera, *Liturgy and Spirituality*, p. 60.

87 There must be clear distinction between those with mere psychic manifestations and genuine charismatic possessions.

88 Cf. *SC*. nr. 24.

89 Cf. Patrick C. Chibuko, *Paschal Mystery of Christ, Foundation For Liturgical Inculturation in Africa*, Peter Lang, Europaeisher Verlag der Wissenschaften, Vol. 120, Frankfurt am, 1999, reprinted by SNAAP Press Nigeria, Ltd., 2001, p. 22.

90 Cf. *Ibid.*

91 Cf. *Ibid.*

[92] Cf. *SC.* 10.

[93] Cf. *Ibid.*

[94] Cf. *Ibid.*

[95] Cf. *Ibid.* p.61-2.

[96] Cf. *Ibid.* p. 62.

[97] Cf. *Ibid.* cf, also, Pope Paul VI, *Apostolic Exhortation Marialis Cultus*, 1974, nos. 16-21; cf. also, I. M. Calabuig, *Spiritualita mariana e spirituality liturgica*, AA. VV., *La Madonna nel culto della Chiesa*, Brescia, 1966, p. 219-40.

[98] Cf. Patrick C. Chibuko, *The Cult of Saints: Beatification to Canonisation of Blessed Cyprian Iwene Tansi*, PAFON Press, Emene Enugu, 2003, p.2-3. Being a Paper presented on the occasion of Transfer of the Remains of the Blessed Tansi for veneration at Enugu, 2003.

[99] Cf. *SC.*, nrr. 104 and 111.

[100] Cf. A. Girolimetto, *Liturgia e vita spirituale: il dibattito sorto negli anni 1913-1914, Liturgia: temi e autori. Saggi di studio sul movimento liturgico*, ed. F. Brovelli, Roma, 1990, 211-74; cf. also, A. M. Triacca, *La riscoperta della liturgia*, AA. VV., *la spiritualita come teologia*, Roma, 1993, p. 105-30; in Jesu Castellano Cervera, *Liturgy and Spirituality...*, p. 54.

[101] Cf. *SC.* nr. 13.

[102] For an elaborate explanation regarding the need for the Regulation of the Sacred Liturgy see, *Redemptionis Sacramentum - On Certain Matters to be Observed or to be Avoided Regarding the Most Holy Eucharist*, Congregation for Divine Worship and the Discipline of the Sacraments, Rome, Solemnity of the Annunciation of the Lord 25th March, 2004, nrr. 14-35. (Signed by the Prefect, Francis Cardinal Arinze and the Archbishop Secretary, Domenico Sorrentino.

[103] Cf. *SC.* nrr. 22-23; cf. also nr. 38.

[104] Cf. *SC.* nr. 5; cf. also, St. Ignatius of Antioch: *Ad Ephesios*, 7:2.; 1 Tim. 2:5.

[105] Cf. Jn. 10:16:...*Ofu onye nche atulu na ofu igwe atulu* (Igbo translation). Christ left only one Peter with a bunch of keys. The church has to insist in her teaching and celebration on one Peter with the bunch of keys. If Christ were to send heavenly church censoring Angels, (equivalent to Nigerian NAFDAC) it is most likely that the proliferation of churches will be a thing of the past. Can there be unity of hearts with divergent thoughts, doctrines and liturgies?

[106] For an extensive study of ancestrology in the liturgy, see Patrick C. Chibuko, *Paschal Mystery of Christ...*, p.96-9.

[107] Cf. J. M. Ela, *My Faith as an African*, Geoffrey Chapman- Cassel Publishers, London, 1989, p.16.

[108] Cf. L. N. Mbefo, *Towards a Mature African Christianity*, SNAAP Press, Enugu, 1989, p. 67. As for the inclusion of women in ancestorship and the role of women in African

development, cf. A. Echema, *Corporate Personality in Traditional Igbo Society and Sacrament of Reconciliation*, Peter Lang, Frankfurt, 1995, p.32.

109 Cf. B. Bujo, *Ahnenkult in Afrika*, in: H. Waldenfels, ed, Lexikon der Religionen, p. 16-17.

110 *Liturgical Piety*, University of Notre Dame Press, Notre Dame, 1955, p. 267.

111 Cf. Langdon Gilkey, *Addressing God in Faith*, in: *Concilium* 82(1973).

112 The problem of meaning of the word, *Missa* is definitively and profoundly studied by Ch. Mohrmann, in: *Vigiliae Christianae*, 12, 1958, p. 67-92 and currently contained in: A. Nocent a cura di, *Storia della Celebrazione dell' Eucaristia, in: Anamnesis 3/2- La Liturgia, Eucaristia, Teologia e Storia della Celebrazione,* a cura di: Salvatore Marsili, Adrian Nocent, Matias Auge and Anscar J. Chupungco, Casa Editrice Marietti, Casale Monferrato, 1983, p. 187 - 190.

Chapter Three: Ite Missa Est - Go the Mass is Ended!

113 Cf. Etherie, *Journal de voyage*, ed. E. Petre, in: *Sources chretiennes*, 21; see especially 28, 2-30, 2, 3; 37, 1, 7-9; 46, 6, etc.

114 Cf. St. Benedict, *The Rule of the Monks,* 17.

115 Cf. *Ibidem,* 38.

116 Fore-Mass refers to the period of the early Church when catechumens are dismissed immediately after the liturgy of the word. They are sent away for the second part of the celebration which is the Eucharist, with the same term, *Missa* for dismissal.

117 Cf. Joseph A. Jungmann, *The Mass of the Roman Rite: Its Origin and Development (Missarum Sollemnia)*, Francis A. Brunner, trans. Volume 2, Christian Classics, Westminster Maryland, 1986, p. 432 - 3; cf. also Lucien Deiss, *The Mass*, Lucien Deiss and Michael S. Driscoll, trans., The Liturgical Press, Collegeville, Minnesota, 1992, p. 102.

118 cf. *Ibid.*

119 Cf. Lucien Deiss, *The Mass,* p. 102.

120 Some early authors like Doelger concludes that the formula must have been in use already in the year 400, but that a dismissal with this or an almost similar formula must already be presumed in Tertullian, cf. *de an*, c. 9 (*CSEL* 20, 310, when he says of the end of the Mass: *post transacta sollemnia dimissa plebe* - after celebrating the Mass, the people are dismissed, in: J. A. Jungmann.

121 Again senate sessions at the time of the Roman Republic were concluded with the words *Nemo vos tenet* - no one holds you back. The Committees at the time of the emperor were dismissed with *Nihil vos moramur, patres conscripti* - we delay you for nothing, you elected or assembled fathers. Livy, 11, 56, 12 gives the dismissal formula given by the tribune: *Si vobis videtur, discedite Quirites* - If it seems proper or right to you, go you Roman Commonwealth of Quirite citizens or you the Roman nation of Quirites. Roman Quirites was the combined name for Romans after their unification.

122 A city state of Umbria region in Italy now known as Gubbio City.

123 Cf. R. Cabie, *Eucharist*, in: A. G. Martimort, ed., *The Church at Prayer*, vol. 11, The Liturgical Press, Collegeville - Minnesota, 1986, p. 123.

124 Both at High Mass and Low Mass, *Ite missa est* was used.

125 Cf. Jn. 1:39.

126 Cf. Matt. 28:19; Mk. 16:15.

127 The problem today is that there seems to be to many go, go, go, with very few come, come, come.

128 It is being suggested especially in the mission lands like Igboland of Nigeria, whether an alternative dismissal formula like *Missa agwusigo Nodinu n'udo* - Mass is ended stay put in peace or remain in peace on special occasions when the assembly is expected to remain behind for the uninterrupted continuation of other important part of the occasion immediately after the Mass.

129 cf. Jn. 1:14; Gal. 4:4; Philippians 2: 6ff.

130 Our politicians must be able to provide what the people need: food to the hungry, water to the thirsty, medicare, create favourable and enabling environment for people to develop and maximise their potentialities for the progress of the people, security, education, job opportunities, stable economy etc. for those politicians asking for second term in office, their past performance should be the criteria for re-election. You promised to give food, water, electricity, job opportunities, roads. Are these already in place to qualify you for a second term?

131 In the middle thirties of this century unemployment invaded many respectable and decent homes. The father's skill was rusting in idleness: the mother was trying to make a shilling do what a pound ought to do; children could not understand what was going one except that they were hungry. Men grew bitter or broken. To go and tell such people that material things make no difference was unforgivable, especially if the teller was in reasonable comfort himself. A General in the army, was once blamed for offering food and meals to poor people instead of the simple gospel. The old warrior flashed back, it is impossible to comfort people's hearts with the love of God when their feet are perishing with cold.
Mother Theresa of Calcutta gave a golden principle with the poor lot of the Indian ghettos. She first fed the poor people with bodily nourishment, bandaged their wounds and soothed their bodily pains and later asked them whether they would like to hear about Christ and the love for his kingdom. One of them asked her, who is Christ, is he as good as you are? She answered, all I am doing, I learnt from him. They answered, please go ahead and tells us more about him.

132 cf. William Barclay, *The Daily Study Bible, The Gospel of Luke*, Revised Edition, The Saint Andrew Press, Edinburgh, 1977, p.115-6.

133 cf. James L. Empereur and Christopher G. Kiesling, *The Liturgy That Does Justice*, A Michael Glazier Book, The Liturgical Press, Collegeville, Minnesota, Theology and Life Series, vol. 33, 1990, p. 6-7.

[134] A just liturgy is not one which is celebrated by and for gay-lesbians, women, blacks and I add, HIV/Aids victims, or any other oppressed group, but which manipulates symbols, confusing them with signs, creating an imbalance by reducing the total prayer experience to an one dimensional attempt to achieve some political action as a result of the liturgical celebration. Nor is liturgy just if it becomes the opportunity for some angry, conflicted people to avoid the expense of psychotherapy by engaging in free group sensitivity, dominating the ritual with personal agenda. Cf. *Ibid.*, p. 18.

[135] Cf. *Ibid.*, p. 19.

[136] Cf. *Ibid.*

[137] Cf. *Ibid.*

[138] *Economic Justice For All: Catholic Social Teaching and the U. S. Economy*, Washington, D. C.: National Conference of Catholic Bishops, in Origins 16:24, November 27, 1986, nr 329.

[139] Cf. *Ibid.*, nr. 330.

[140] Cf. *Ibid.*, nr. 331.

[141] Cf. *Economic Justice For All: Catholic Social Teaching And The U.S. Economy,* Washington D. C. USCC, June, 1986, Sections 325 and 326.

[142] Cf. . James L. Empereur and Christopher G. Kiesling, , p. 232.

[143] Cf. *Ibid.*

[144] Cf. Ronald J. Wilkins, *Achieving Social Justice, A christian Perspective*, Religious Education Division, Wm. C. Brown Company, Publishers, Dubuque, Iowa, 1980, p. 9-10.

[145] Cf. *The Liturgy That Does Justice, Social Justice in the Liturgy of the Eucharist*, p. 109ff.

[146] Cf. *Ibid.*

[147] Cf. Barbara Beckwith, *Why Sexist Language Doesn't Belong in Church (or Anywhere Else)*, St Anthony Messenger 88 (February 1981) 22-26; Jacky Kelly, *The Justice of Inclusive Language, Modern Liturgy* 11:5 (June/July/August, 1984)27; Carol Schuck, *Christians Shouldn't Use Sexist Language*, U. S. Catholic 49 (April, 1984), 12- 13, in: James L. Empereur and Christopher G. Kiesling, *The Liturgy That Does Justice, Social Justice in the Liturgy of the Eucharist*, p. 111- 112.

[148] Cf. *Ibid.* p. 115-116.

[149] *Eucharistic Prayer 1* for instance prays thus: we offer them for your Holy Catholic Church.... grant it peace and unity through out the world; *Eucharistic Prayer 11*, says: May all who share in the Body and Blood of Christ be brought together in unity by the Holy Spirit; *Eucharistic Prayer 111*, re-echoes the same intention though slightly different saying: Grant that we, who are nourished by his Body and Blood, may be filled with the Holy Spirit and become one body, one spirit in Christ. These remind us also of the christian unity which Christ prayed for in Jn. 17: 21-23; cf. also Gal. 3:27-28; Col. 3:11; 1 Cor. 12:4-6,14-30; Rom. 12:3-8; Eph. 4:11, 16.

150 For instance are women treated more justly in the church than in secular society? Does the church serve as a model to the world for the treatment of minorities? Is the church a leader in the way it provides for disabled persons etc.?

151 Cf. Xavier Leon-Dufour, ed. *Dictionary of Biblical Theology,* Desclee, New York, 1967, p.364-65.

152 Cf. Michael J. Himes, *Doing the Truth in Love: Conversations about God, Relationships and Servi*ce, Paulist Press, New York, 1995, p. 118.

153 Cf. *Ecclesia in America*, nr. 55.

154 Such as the stock market, the World Trade Organisation, energy policy, sweatshops, AIDS, drugs, racial, religious and ethnic conflicts, immigration, arms trade and global warming are defining our globe.

Chapter Four: Eucharistic Liturgy, The Undying Hope of the Church

155 By mystical body is meant, Christ the Head and members of his Body, the Church.

156 The Paschal Mystery of Christ can be well understood in the broad and narrow senses. In the broad sense, it includes the incarnation, the birth, the public life, the ministry, the miracles, the doctrines, the passion, death, resurrection, ascension, Pentecost, sitting at the right hand of God and the final coming of Christ in glory. That would mean the totality of what Christ is. Secondly, it has a very close connection with the entirety of the christian mystery which is summarised in the Church's creed: the Holy Trinity, creation, fall, redemption, sanctification, grace, Mariology, sanctorals, sacraments, death, judgement, heaven, hell. It remains the central and focal point of all that the Church believes and celebrates. The strict sense of the term includes simply, the passion, death and resurrection of Christ.

157 Every liturgical celebration reaches its apex or summit in the Eucharist. At the same time every celebration draws its strength and nourishment from the Eucharist.

158 Some of these include Dedication of Churches, Altars etc.

159 Letter of St. Paul to the Romans 12:1.

160 Catholics belong to the Church that possesses in full all that one needs to believe in, for salvation.

161 The allusion here is not *in Jesus name because this is not biblical and it is also not catholic as well as against the Catholic liturgical tradition.* Catholics do not begin prayer in Jesus name, they rather end up with Jesus Christ, the one who was born of the Virgin Mary, suffered, died and rose and now seated at the right hand of the Father, making intercessions for the Church and the world while continuing his priestly function of intercession and mediation.

162 Jesus is the Greek form by which three Hebrew Old Testament names are regularly represented - Joshua in Ex. 17:10; Jehoshua in Zech. 3:1; Jeshua in Neh. 7:7. There are indeed two occasions in which Joshua is very confusingly called Jesus in AA. 7:45 and Heb. 4:8. In both cases Jesus is Joshua, a fact which is made clear in all the more modern translations.

Furthermore, in New Testament times the name Jesus was one of the commonest of names. There was Jesus Justus, the friend of Paul (Col. 4:11), the sorcerer of Paphos is called Bar-Jesus (AA 13:6). There were at least five High Priests who were called Jesus.

In the works of the historian Josephus there appear about twenty people called Jesus, ten of whom were contemporary with Jesus Christ. One of the best known and most important books of the Apocrypha, the book usually known by the name Ecclesiasticus, is the work of Jesus the son of Sirach.

In the contemporary census and taxation returns found among the papyri the name Jesus often occurs. A very interesting possible occurrence of the name Jesus is in Matt. 27:18.

There are certain manuscripts which give Jesus as the first name of Barabbas. The RSV notes this reading...where Pilate asked the people, which would you like me to release to you - Jesus Bar-Abbas, or Jesus called Messiah.

By the second century the name Jesus was vanishing as an ordinary name. Amongst the Jews it vanished because it had become a hated name by which no Jew would call his son; and amongst the Christians it had vanished because it was too sacred for common use, cf. William Barclay, *Jesus As They Saw Him, New Testament Interpretations of Jesus,* SCM Press, Ltd., 1977, pp. 9-13.

[163] Cf. Lk. 24:6.

[164] Cf. Lk. 2: 41-50.

[165] Cf. Mtt. 18:20.

[166] Cf. Jn. 4:34.

[167] Cf. *Instruction, Redemptionis Sacramentum, On Certain Matters To Be Observed Or To Be Avoided Regarding The Most Holy Eucharist,* (henceforth *Redemptionis Sacramentum* or *RS*) Congregation For Divine Worship And The Discipline of the Sacraments (henceforth *CDWDS*), 23rd April, 2004, nr. 5; cf. also, Missale Romanum, Prex Eucharistica III, p. 588, cf. also I Cor. 12:12-13; Eph. 4:4; cf. also Phil. 2:5.

[168] Cf. *SC.* nr. 9.

[169] Cf. *SC.* nr. 10.

[170] Cf. *SC.* nr. 14.

[171] Cf. *SC.* nr. 34.

[172] Cf. *SC.* nr 22:3

[173] Cf. *SC.* nr. 38.

[174] Cf. *SC.* nrr. 77-78.

[175] Cf. Pope John Paul II, *Vicesimus Quintus Annus,* 4th Dec. 1988, nr. 4:

[176] Cf. Pope's Letter through Cardinal Angelo Sodano, Secretary of State to Bishop Adriano Caprioli of Reggio Emilia-Gustala, Italy, President of the Episcopal Commission for the Liturgy, *Council's Reforms Must Be Part of Believers' Lives, L'Osservatore Romano,* nr. 39, 24th Septermber 2003.

[177] Cf. *Ibid.*

[178] Cf. *Ibid.*

[179] Cf. *Ibid.*

[180] Cf. *CIC*, can. 1055 para. 1; cf. *GS.* 48 para. 1.

[181] Cf. D. G. Dix, *The Shape of the Liturgy*, A. and C. Black, London, 1986, p. 22-24.

[182] Cf. A. J. Chupungco, *Cultural Adaptation of the Liturgy*, Paulist Press, New York, 1982, 18-19.

[183] Cf. *Ibid.*, p. 23 –24.

[184] Cf. *Ibid.*, 23 –24.

[185] Cf. A. Nocent, *The Liturgical Year*, vol. 2., The Liturgical Press, Collegeville, 1971, p. 203-214.

[186] Cf. *SC.* Nr. 10: Incidentally, this was the phrase used by the liturgical reformers of the Second Vatican Council to describe the nature of the liturgy, which applies also particularly to the Eucharist as the chief act of liturgy.

[187] Cf. *CCC*. nr. 1343, 2177.

[188] Cf. *CCC*. nr. 1212.

[189] Cf. *Ibid.*, nr. 1322.

[190] Cf. *Ibid.* nr. 1440.

[191] Cf. *Ibid.* nr. 1487.

[192] Cf. *Ibid.* nr. 1499; cf also Jas. 5:14-16; Rom. 8:17; Col. 1:24; 2 Tim. 2:11-12, 1 Pet. 4:13.

[193] Cf. *Ibid.* nr. 1536.

[194] Cf. Patrick C. Chibuko, *Paschal Mystery of Christ, Foundation for Liturgical Inculturation in Africa,* Peter Lang Verlag, Frankfurt, 1999, p. 139.

[195] Cf. Heb.8:4; *CCC.* Nr. 1545.

[196] Cf. *CIC*, can. 1055 para. 1; cf. *GS.* 48 para. 1.

[197] Cf. Peter J. Elliot, *Liturgical Question Box, Answers To Common Questions About the Liturgy*, Ignatius Press, San Francisco, 1998, p. 14.

[198] Cf. *Ibid.*, p. 15.

[199] Cf. *CIC*, Canon 528 para. 2.

[200] Cf. *Instruction, Redemptionis Sacramentum,* nrr. 1-5.

[201] Cf. *Ibid.*, nrr. 6-10.

[202] Cf. *Ibid.*, nr. 183.

[203] Cf. *Ibid.*, nr. 184.

[204] Cf. *Ibid.*, nr. 186.

Chapter Five: Liturgical Preaching:

205 Numerous works have appeared in the recent past regarding the problematics involved in today's preaching. Most of these include, Patricia A. Parachini, *Lay Preaching, State of the Question, American Essays in Liturgy*, A Liturgical Press Book, The Liturgical Press, Collegeville, Minnesota, 1999, (pp. 3-68). Confer also. J. Frank Henderson, *The Minister of Liturgical Preaching, Worship* 56(1982) (216ff.), James H. Provost, *Lay Preaching and Canon Law in a Time of Transition, Preaching and the Non-Ordained*, ed., Nadine Foley, Liturgical Press, Collegeville, 1983, (p. 139); cf. John Burke and Thomas P. Doyle, *The Homilist's Guide to Scripture, Theology and Canon Law*, Pueblo Publishers, New York, 1987, (chapter 5)., John M. Huels, *Lay Preaching at Liturgy, More Disputed Questions in the Liturgy*, Liturgy Training Publications, Chicago, 1996, (189).

206 Cf. *Dogmatic Constitution On Divine Revelation, Die Verbum*, nr. 21. cf. also nr. 1329.

207 Cf. *SC*. nr. 15.

208 Cf. Domenico Sartore, C.S.J., *The Homily*, in: *Handbook for Liturgical Studies, The Eucharist*, (ed. Anscar J. Chupungco, vol. 3., A Pueblo Book, The Liturgical Press, Collegeville Minnesota, 1997, pp. 189-208.

209 cf. *Ibid*.

210 Cf. R. Gregoire, *Omelia*, in: *Dizionario patristico e di atichita cristiane*, vol. 2, 1983, pp. 2467-2472.

211 Cf. Augustine, *Epistle* 224, 2 (opere di. S. Augustino XXII), Rome 1974, p. 650. It says inter alia, *tractatus populares, quos Graeci homilias vocant*; cf. also C. Mohrmann, *Praedicare-Tractare-Sermo*, Etudes sur le latin des chretiens, 11, Rome, 1961, 63-72.

212 Cf. Justin Martyr, *1 Apologia*, 67, 3-5, in: A. Haenggi - I Pahl, *Prex eucharistica*, (SF 12), Freiburg/Switzerland 1968, , 70-1 (Greek and Latin text).

213 Cf. Domenico Sartore, , *The Homily*, p. 190.

214 Cf. *Ibid*., p. 190-191.

215 Cf. *Ibid*., p. 191.

216 Cf. Rom. 10:17.

217 Cf. *Ibid*.

218 Melito of Sardis, *Sur la Paque et fragments, Sources Chretiennes*, (hence forth *SChr*) Paris, 1966, 123, as cited in: Domenico Sartore, *The Homily*, p. 191.

219 R. Cantalamessa, *L'omelia in Sanctum Pascha dello pseudo-Ippolito di Roma*, Milan, 1966, p. 434.

220 Cf. *Ibid*.

221 Cf. J. Leclercq, Le sermon, act liturgique, in: *La Maison Dieu (MD)* 8 (1946) 27-47; see also *Liturgie et les paradoxes chretiens (LO 36)*, Paris 1963, p. 208.

[222] Cf. *Ibid.*, p. 210.

[223] Cf. *Ibid.*, 211-212.

[224] Cf. Domenico Sartore, *The Homily,* p. 193.

[225] Cf. *Ibid.*, nr. 22.

[226] Cf. *SC*. nr. 24.

[227] Cf. *Ibid.*

[228] Cf. J. A. Jungmann, *Konstitution ueber die heilige Liturgie. Enleitung und Kommenta,* in: *Lexikon fuer Theologie und Kirche,* Freiburg, (1957-1966), Band III, 54-55; cf. also, Sacred Congregation for Rites, hence forth *SCR, Instructio Inter oecumenici ad executionem constitutionis de sacra Liturgia recte ordinandam, AAS* 56 (1964) 877-900: nn. 53-55.

[229] Cf. *SC*. nr. 24.

[230] Cf. *SC*. nr. 35:2.

[231] Cf. *SC*. 52.

[232] Cf. Instruction *Inter Oecumenici,* nr. 53.

[233] Cf. *Ibid.*, nr. 54.

[234] Cf. *Ibid.*, nr. 55.

[235] Cf. *Missale Romanum* ex decreto Sacrosancti Oecimenici Concilii Vaticanis 11 instauratum, auctoritate Pauli PP. Promulgatum, ed. Typica altera, 1975: *Institutio Generalis* nr. 42.

[236] Cf. *Ordo Lectionum Missae (OLM),* 1969, nr. 24.

[237] Paulus PP. VI, *Adhortatio Apostolica Evangelii Nuntiandi de Evangelizatione in Mundo huius Temporis,* nr. 43, *AAS* 58 (1976) 1008-125.

[238] Cf. *Ibid.*

[239] Cf. John Paul II, *Adhortatio Apostolica Catechesi Tradendae,* nr. 48, *AAS* 71 (1979) 1277-340.

[240] Cf. *Ibid.*

[241] Cf. Sacred Congregation for the Clergy, *General Catechetical Directory*, Turin (Leumann) 1971, nr.71.

[242] Cf. D. Grasso, *Evangelizzazione, Catechesi, Omelia,Gregorianum* 42(1961)242-267. See also, Conferenza Episcopale Italiana (hence forth CEI), *Il rinnovamento della catechesi*, Rome, 1970, nrr. 22.

[243] Cf.CEI, *Il rinnovamento....*nr. 29.

[244] Cf. *SC*. nr. 52.

[245] Cf. St. Leo the Great, *Sermo 61, de Ascensione Domini:* SChr 74, p. 278.

[246] Cf. Domenico Sartore, *The Homily,* p.201.

[247] Cf. *Ibid.*

[248] Cf. *OLM*, **Editio Typica Altera**, 1981, nr. 3.

[249] Cf. *Instituto Generalis Missale Romanum, General Instruction of the Roman Missal of Paul VI* nr. 41.

[250] Cf. F. Dreyfus, *L'actualisation a l'interieur de la Bible, Revue Biblique (RB)*, Paris, (1892-)

[251] Cf. E. Lodi, *Aspetti sociologici dell'Omelia, Revista Liturgica (RL)* 52 (1970)584-614.

[252] Cf. Sacred Congregation For Divine Worship, *Liturgiae Instaurationes, 5 September, 1970, no. 2ab.*

[253] Cf. *Omelia, Enciclopedia di Pastorale, 3, Liturgia,* Casale Montferrato, 1988, p. 170-175.

[254] Cf. Patricia A. Parachini, *Lay Preaching, State of the Question,* p. 44.

[255] Cf. *Ibid.*

[256] Cf. John M. Huels, *Lay Preaching at Liturgy,* p. 183-4.

[257] Cf. Patricia A. Parachini, *Lay Preaching, State of the Question,* p. 45.

[258] The moments include at the beginning of the Eucharistic celebration, at the Gospel and at the end of the celebration..

[259] Cf. Erasto J. Fernandez, *The Eucharist Step by Step,* St. Paul's Publication, Bombay, 1994, p. 52.

[260] Cf. *Ibid.*

[261] Cf. Lucien Deiss, *The Mass,* The Liturgical Press, Collegeville, Minnesota, 1992, p.41.

[262] Cf. *Thanksgiving to Origen,* XV, 179, quoted in Lucien Deiss, *The Mass...,* p.42. .

[263] Cf. *SC.* 41. Cf. also *SC. 42* for the recommended days on which homilies are most suitable, namely, Sundays and holidays of obligation. Others include the weekdays of Advent, Lent and Eastertide and on liturgical occasions where there is a large number of people.

[264] Cf. Sacred Congregation For Divine Worship, *Liturgiae Instaurationes, 5 September, 1970, no. 2ab.*

[265] Cf. AA. 6:2.

[266] Cf. Adolf Adam, *The Liturgical Year, Its History and Its Meaning After the Reforms of the Liturgy,* Pueblo Publications Co., New York, 1981, p. 19.

[267] Cf. Gabriel M. Braso, *Liturgy and Spirituality,* translated by Leonard J. Doyle, The Liturgical Press, St. John's Abbey, Collegeville, Minnesota, 1971, p. 290.

[268] Cf. nrr.1534.

[269] Cf. Council of Trent, Denzinger Schoenmezer nr. 1799.

[270] Cf. *SC.* 61; *Lumen Gentium,* nr. 6, based on 1 Cor. 10:17.

[271] Cf. *Order of Christian Funerals,* nr. 141.

272 Cf. Peter J. Elliot, *Liturgical Question Box, Answers To Common Questions About the Liturgy*, Ignatius Press, San Francisco, 1998, p. 183ff.

273 Cf. *Ibid*. p. 184.

274 Cf. J. O. Awolalu, *Sin and its Removal in African Traditional Religion*, in: Journal of the American Academy of Religion, 44 (1976) p. 275 –282.

275 Cf. L. V. Thomas and R. Luneau, *Les Religions d' Afrique noire*, vol. 1 (Paris: Stock and Plus, 198) 28 cited in: Elochukwu E. Uzukwu, *Worship As Body Language*, p. 271.

276 Cf. *Ibid*.

277 Chinua Achebe, *Things Fall Apart*, Heinemann Educational Books, London – Ibadan – Nairobi, 1973, p. 51. This was the message brought to Okonkwo, the custodian of a lad, Ikemefuna who was brought from Mbaino, the neighbouring village together with a virgin girl in exchange for their killing of a daughter of Umuofia. In order to avert an imminent war between the two towns, the Mbaino people placated their angry neighbour who were bent on revenge through war by offering the boy and the girl. But as the custom states, his blood must be shed but not until the Oracle of the Hills and the Caves has pronounced it. This was the fate that befell the innocent Ikemefuna. After his gruesome death the sad story is still being told in Umuofia unto this day.

278 Cf. Erasto J. Fernandez, *The Eucharist Step by Step*, p. 55.

279 Cf. *Ibid*.

280 The list was very much limited when it was first given by Rev. Prof. A. Akubue at the priests retreat in the nineties. The author has not only increased the list but has fleshed it up in a more scientific form.

281 The nature of liturgy demands the use of refined proverbs as some of the local proverbs are obnoxious and unsuitable for a refined assembly as the liturgy. Today incidentally, some of them have been refined such as *Egbe belu ugo belu, nke si ibe ya ebena, gosi ya ebe oga ebe* instead of *nke si ibe ya ebena nku kwapu ya.*

282 Tortoise stories must be told with prudence because of what the animal represents in most of the stories. Often it represents trickery, lies, etc. more harm could be done by telling tortoise stories especially to children indiscriminately. One could end up enthroning the vice of trickery, cheating and lies.

283 Cf. Peter J. Elliot, *Ceremonies of the Modern Roman Rite,* nr. 209, p. 76.

284 Cf. Karl Rahner, *The Shape of the Church to Come*, Edward Quinn, trans. The Seabury Press, New York, 1974, p. 87quoted in Patricia A. Parachini, *Lay Preaching*, ...p. 59.

285 Cf. Patricia A. Parachini, *Lay Preaching*, ...p. 59.

General Conclusion:

286 Cf. *Ibid.,* nr. 11.

287 Cf. *Ibid.,* nr.12.

IKO – Verlag
für Interkulturelle Kommunikation

Patrick Chukwudezie
Chibuko
**Keeping the Liturgy
alive**
An Anglophone West
African Experience
192 S., € 16,90,
ISBN 3-88939-704-2

"This work presents a passionate case for the rehabilitation of authentic liturgy in the church within the West African sub-region. Therefore the author calls for serious attention to liturgy and the intellectual formation of liturgical actors."

Patrick Chukwudezie
Chibuko
**Liturgical
Inculturation**
An authentic African
Response
194 S., € 14,80,
ISBN 3-88939-636-4

"The positive role of worship in the struggle for freedom, justice and peace is quite enormous. True worship is not an anaesthetic frivolous diversion of energy from the battles for development and fair play. It is an announcement to all tyrants ..."

"The Catholic Church in Nigeria, represented by the bishops, has to act here as the conscience of the State by means of critique and work for the respect of the fundamental rights of the citizens and the well-being of the human person."

John Chidi Nwafor
**Church and State:
The Nigerian Experience**
The relationship between the Church and the State in Nigeria in the areas of Human Rights, Education, Religious Freedom and Religious Tolerance
Ethik, Gesellschaft, Wirtschaft, Vol. 13
444 S., € 26,80, ISBN 3-88939-632-1

"...this book offers an interesting and inspiring study of Igbo traditional initiation forms in comparison with the Christian sacraments of initiation."

George Nnaemeka Oranekwu
**The Significant Role of Initiation
in the Traditional Igbo
Culture and Religion**
An Inculturation Basis for Pastoral
Catechesis of Christian Initiation
Ezi Muoma – Afrika verstehen, Vol. 2
268 S., € 21,80, ISBN 3-88939-710-7

www. iko-verlag.de – find all current titles – visit us!